HITCHCOCK'S FILMS

Alfred Hitchcock's more than fifty films have given him the reputation of being the master of suspense. Yet to the film buff, Hitchcock's films are more than mere suspense-thrillers. They are examples of "pure cinema." For Hitchcock not only makes his audience "see"—he makes them "feel." It is for this reason—his unusual and total technique—that Hitchcock deserves serious study by every student of cinema art.

#2 —International Film Guide Series

HITCHCOCK'S FILMS

by Robin Wood

Edited by Peter Cowie

PAPERBACK LIBRARY

New York

PAPERBACK LIBRARY EDITION

First Printing: September, 1970

Copyright © 1965, 1969 by Robin Wood

Library of Congress Catalog Card Number: 69-14903

ACKNOWLEDGEMENTS

STILLS are reproduced by courtesy of the following: Warner Bros. *(Stage Fright, I Confess, Strangers on a Train, The Wrong Man)*; Paramount *(Vertigo, Psycho)*; M.G.M. *(Rope, North by Northwest)*; The Rank Organisation *(The Birds, Marnie, Torn Curtain)*; and the National Film Archive (all other illustrations).

I am greatly indebted to Peter Harcourt and Alan Lovell of the Education Department of the British Film Institute for generous assistance with this project. I wish to thank David Francis of the National Film Archive for arranging for me to see certain films otherwise unavailable, and the staff of the Archive itself at Aston Clinton for their kindness and hospitality during my visit. For various useful ideas, suggestions and criticisms I am indebted to Charles Barr, James Leahy, John Cant and Frances Harman. Finally I wish to express my deep gratitude to my wife (to whom this book is dedicated) for not only stoically enduring six months of unmitigated Hitchcock but also supporting and encouraging the enterprise throughout; without her the book would never have been written.

This Paperback Library Edition is published by arrangement with A. S. Barnes & Co., Inc.

CONTENTS

1. INTRODUCTION   7
2. STRANGERS ON A TRAIN   47
3. REAR WINDOW   65
4. VERTIGO   76
5. NORTH BY NORTHWEST   106
6. PSYCHO   121
7. THE BIRDS   134
8. MARNIE   163
9. TORN CURTAIN   195
    Filmography of Alfred Hitchcock   208
    Bibliography   222

HITCHCOCK'S FILMS
by Robin Wood

1. Introduction

WHY SHOULD WE take Hitchcock seriously?

It is a pity the question has to be raised: if the cinema were truly regarded as an autonomous art, not as a mere adjunct of the novel or the drama—if we were able yet to *see* films instead of mentally reducing them to literature —it would be unnecessary. As things are, it seems impossible to start a book on Hitchcock without confronting it.

Hitchcock has expressed repeatedly his belief in "pure cinema"; to appreciate his films it is necessary that we grasp the nature of the medium. We are concerned here with much more than is normally meant by the word "technique". Let us look at an example.

In *Marnie* Mark Rutland (Sean Connery) tries to "persuade" Strutt (Martin Gabel) not to take action against Marnie for robbing him (the money has been returned). Strutt protests that the lenient attitude asked of him is "fashionable", but "just wait till *you've* been victimized". Then we see Marnie enter the house. She has just been through a terrible accident, has had to shoot her beloved horse, still carries the pistol in her hand: she is distraught, and quite bereft of free will or the power of rational consideration. Reduce this to literary "content" detached from the images (from the movement of the images, and the movement from image to image) and there isn't much there: a straightforward dramatic situation with a rather dislikeable man making things unpleasant for the poor heroine. But compare this account with the force of the images on the screen. The cut from Strutt to Marnie gives us, first, an ironic comment on Strutt's word "victimized". We see Strutt, complacent, self-righteous, a man devoid of human warmth and generosity taking his stand on a rigid, standardised morality; then we see Marnie, haggard, drawn, face drained of all colour, clinging to a gun without realizing she is holding

7

it, moving forward like a sleepwalker, "victimized" indeed by a whole complex past. It defines for us our moral attitude to Strutt's moral attitude, and is a comment on Strutt himself and all he stands for (he stands, in the film, for quite a lot: a whole attitude to life, a whole social milieu). There is also colour: Mark wears a brown-flecked tweed suit and a brown tie, so that he blends naturally with the "natural" colours—predominantly browns and greens—of the décor of the Rutland house: the hard blue of Strutt's tie clashes with the green of the sofa on which he is sitting, making him out of place in the décor as his attitude to life is out of place in the Rutland milieu. The point, like so much that is important in the film, is *felt* rather than registered consciously by the spectator.

A novelist could give us some kind of equivalent for all this, could make us react along the same general lines; but he couldn't make us react in this direct, immediate way, as image succeeds image—he couldn't control our reactions so precisely in time. He could describe the way Strutt was sitting, but he couldn't *show* us Strutt sitting in precisely that way: we would all imagine it differently. He couldn't place us at a certain distance from Strutt to watch his awkwardness, his gestures, his changing expressions from a slightly low angle, so that we are aware at once of his absurdity and of his power. He could describe Marnie's appearance and analyse explicitly her emotional state from within (as Hitchcock can't); he couldn't show us her face, her way of moving; he couldn't place us above her, so that we look down on her with compassion; he couldn't place us in front of her and make us move with her, at her speed, so that we are caught up in her rhythm of moving, so that we share for a moment her trance-like state. The novelist can analyse and explain; Hitchcock can make us experience directly.

I have purposefully chosen here a quite unremarkable (in its context) example which contains nothing obviously "cinematic": it could be paralleled from almost any sequence in *Marnie*. It seems to me a fair representative specimen of that local realisation that one finds everywhere in recent Hitchcock films, realisation of theme in terms of "pure cinema" which makes the audience not only see but *experience* (experience rather than intellectually analyse) the manifestation of that theme at that particular point.

Or consider the moment in *Psycho* when Norman Bates carries his mother down to the fruit-cellar. In literary terms there is almost nothing there: a young man carrying a limp body out of a room and down some stairs. Yet in the film the overhead shot with its complicated camera-movement communicates to us precisely that sense of metaphysical vertigo that Hitchcock's subject requires at that moment: a sense of sinking into a quicksand of uncertainties, or into a bottomless pit: communicates it by placing us in a certain position in relation to the action and controlling our movements in relation to the movements of the actors. The cinema has its own methods and its own scope. We must beware of missing the significance of a shot or a sequence by applying to it assumptions brought from our experience of other arts.

The cinema—especially the Hollywood cinema—is a commercial medium. Hitchcock's films are—usually—popular: indeed, some of his best films (*Rear Window, Psycho*) are among his *most* popular. From this arises a widespread assumption that, however "clever", "technically brilliant", "amusing", "gripping", etc., they may be, they can't be taken seriously as we take, say, the films of Bergman or Antonioni seriously. They *must* be, if not absolutely bad, at least fatally flawed from a serious standpoint. And it is easy enough for those who take this line to point to all manner of "concessions to the box-office", fatal compromises with a debased popular taste: Hitchcock returns repeatedly to the suspense-thriller for his material; he generally uses established stars who are "personalities" first and actors second; there is a strong element of humour in his work, "gags" and "comic relief" which effectively undermine any pretensions to sustained seriousness of tone. To one whose training has been primarily literary, these objections have a decidedly familiar ring. One recalls that "commercial"—and at the time intellectually disreputable—medium the Elizabethan drama; one thinks of those editors who have wished to remove the Porter scene from *Macbeth* because its tone of bawdy comedy is incompatible with the tragic atmosphere; of Dr. Johnson's complaints about Shakespeare's fondness for "quibbles" and conceits; of Robert Bridges' deploring of the bawdy scenes in such plays as *Measure for Measure*. The argument, in all these cases, was basically much the same: Shakespeare allowed himself these regrettable lapses from high seriousness merely to please the "groundlings"; or, if we can't bear such a thought, we can comfort ourselves with the reflection that perhaps they were interpolations by someone else.

Now, one does not want to deny Shakespeare his imperfections, or Hitchcock his: indeed, a strong objection to much current French exegesis of Hitchcock, as to so much current critical work on Shakespeare, is that the writers tend to start from the assumption that their hero can do no wrong, and quite fail to make necessary discriminations between different works, or admit occasional failures of realisation within works. Such treatment does much harm, by erecting barriers between artist and audience that are very difficult to break down: one is not responding at first hand to a work of art if one approaches it in a spirit of uncritical veneration. But what one does not want either Shakespeare or Hitchcock deprived of is precisely the richness their work derives from the sense of living contact with a wide popular audience. To wish that Hitchcock's films were like those of Bergman or Antonioni is like wishing that Shakespeare had been like Corneille (which is what his eighteenth-century critics *did* wish). This implies no disrespect to Corneille (nor to Bergman and Antonioni) who can offer us experiences that Shakespeare cannot; it is meant to imply that Shakespeare can offer us richer experiences; and that if we somehow removed all trace of "popular" appeal from Shakespeare and Hitchcock, then we would have lost Shakespeare and Hitchcock.

That there are important distinctions to be drawn between Shakespeare's audience and Hitchcock's, and important resulting distinctions between the oeuvres of the two artists, I would not of course wish to deny. And Hollywood is not as conducive to great art as Elizabethan London, for many reasons too obvious to need recounting here. But it is a matter of approaching these alleged concessions and compromises from the right end. I remember once expressing great admiration for Howard Hawks's *Rio Bravo;* I was promptly told that it couldn't be a very good film, because Hawks had used a pop-singer (Ricky Nelson) and then introduced a song-sequence quite arbitrarily to give him something to sing. It didn't apparently occur to the person in question to consider the song-sequence on its own merits in its context in the film (in terms of strict thematic unity it is easier to justify than the role of Autolycus in *The Winter's Tale,* which no one nowadays wishes away, though it represents a "concession to popular taste" that, one feels, delighted Shakespeare's heart very much as the *Rio Bravo* song-sequence delighted Hawks's). It seems clear that the relationship of a Hitchcock or a Hawks to his art is much more like Shakespeare's than is that of a Bergman or an Antonioni; the sense of communication on many levels precludes that self-consciousness of the artist that besets the arts today, and fosters true artistic impersonality. All one asks for Hitchcock is that people *look* at his films, allow themselves to react spontaneously, and consider their reactions; that, for example, instead of assuming that *Vertigo* is just a mystery-thriller (in which case it is a very botched job, with the solution divulged two-thirds of the way through and the rest, one supposes, total boredom), they look without preconceptions at the sequence of images that Hitchcock gives us, and consider their first-hand responses to those images. They will then be led, very swiftly by the straightest path, to the film's profound implications.

It is precisely this refusal to look, react and consider that vitiates most British criticism of Hitchcock's films. The characteristic "Establishment" line may be fairly represented by the article *The Figure in the Carpet* by Penelope Houston in the Autumn 1963 issue of *Sight and Sound:* the immediate stimulus being in this case the appearance in England of *The Birds*. The article is in fact so characteristic, not only of the line on Hitchcock, but of the *Sight and Sound* critical approach in general, that it is worth studying, as a representative document, in some detail: which I do not propose to do here. A few comments, however, seem in order. What is most striking in the article is its almost exclusively negative character. Miss Houston examines cursorily some of the more obvious and easily dismissible excesses both of the book on Hitchcock by Eric Rohmer and Claude Chabrol, and of Jean Douchet's articles in *Cahiers du Cinéma;* when one looks for some clear positive lead one finds almost nothing. Miss Houston appears to include herself in that "general agreement that (Hitchcock) is a master"; yet nothing she finds to say remotely supports such a valuation. There is continual evasion of critical responsibility, a refusal to follow any line of enquiry rigorously to its conclusion. Of *Vertigo* (which Miss Houston seems now to like, though it is impossible to discover why or how much or in what way) we learn that it "hypnotises . . . The first half moves like a slow, underwater dream. The second half . . . has the hallucinatory quality of a nightmare. By the end of the film, the audience ought to be as mad as James Stewart appears to be". And that is all. If we ask for some effort to explain this "hallucinatory quality" —its method, its purpose, its moral implications (for good or ill, intentional or unintentional)—we get no answer from Miss Houston. One is left to assume that any film is vaguely acceptable if it has a "hallucinatory quality".

Most of Miss Houston's article seems to rest on two supports, both critically insufficient to say the least: what Hitchcock has said, and what she herself assumes to have been his intentions in this or that film: and never, as far as one can judge, on a detailed first-hand study of the films themselves. Her closing paragraph (on *The Birds*) is representative: ". . . If *The Birds* is really intended as a doomsday fantasy, one can only say it's a lamentably inadequate one . . ." It is at least equally inadequate if "really intended" as Oedipus Rex, Winnie the Pooh or a pair of kippers: unfortunately, what concerns (or should concern) the critic is not what a film is "really intended" to be, but what it actually *is*. Miss Houston's remark also implies a set notion of what a "doomsday fantasy" ought to be like; anyway, her inability to cope with a complex work like *The Birds* is sufficiently revealed in that desire to package it neatly and tie on a ready-to-hand cliché label. ". . . But why not try the birds as the Bomb; or as creatures from the subconscious; or start from the other end, with Tippi Hedren as a witch? . . ." Why not, indeed? Go ahead, Miss Houston! ". . . One could work up a pretty theory on any of these lines . . ." (Except that a minute's consideration of the film would be enough to show that one couldn't) ". . . if only one could suppress a conviction that Hitchcock's intention . . ." (intention again!) . . . "was an altogether simpler one. He scared us in *Psycho* enough to make us think twice about stopping at any building looking remotely like the Bates motel. He tries it again in *The Birds,* but we will happily go on throwing bread to the seagulls, because the film can't for long enough at a time break through our barrier of disbelief . . ." And one cannot, at this point, suppress a conviction about Miss Houston's conviction: that it existed before she saw *The Birds,* which was accordingly judged by the criterion, Is this frightening me as much (and in the same way?) as *Psycho* frightened me? ". . . And a director who has told us so often that his interest lies in the way of doing things, not in the moral of a story, invites us to take him at his own valuation . . ." An invitation any serious critic ought, one would have supposed, to decline, politely murmuring "Never trust the artist—trust the tale". The whole article—with its apparent assumption

13

that a few odd quirks are enough to justify the description of a director as a master, and one needn't look deeper, needn't at all inquire what this or that film actually *does*— is typical of the dilettantism that vitiates so much British film criticism. One respects far more—while considering them mistaken—those who find Hitchcock's films morally repulsive: at least their attitude is based on the assumption that a work of art (or entertainment) has the power to affect us for good or ill, and that one needs to examine a work in detail and in depth (in Paddy Whannel's words, "teasing out the values embedded in the style") before one can offer any valuation of it. This bland disregard of the need for moral concern (I would say commitment, had the word not become so debased by oversimplification) in some form links up with the astonishing confusion (or absence?) of values revealed by the fact that the issue of *Sight and Sound* that contained Peter John Dyer's contemptuous review of *Marnie* (another interesting representative specimen) also awarded *Goldfinger* three stars in its *Guide to Current Films* ("Films of special interest to *Sight and Sound* readers are denoted by one, two, three or four stars"—do *Sight and Sound* readers accept such blackening of their characters?), and printed Dyer's eulogy of Roger Corman's vulgar and pretentious Bergman plagiarism, *The Masque of the Red Death*.

It is a fact, I think, that the chief obstacle in the way of a serious appraisal of Hitchcock's work for many people is Hitchcock's own apparent attitude to it; and it seems worth insisting for a moment on the fundamental irrelevance of this. What an artist says about his own work need not necessarily carry any more weight than what anyone else says about it: its value can only be assessed by the test to which one must subject all criticism or elucidation, the test of applying it to the art in question and asking oneself how much it contributes towards either understanding or evaluating it. The artist's own utterances are more likely to have an indirect relevance, by telling us something further about his personality and outlook. I used to find maddening Hitchcock's refusal to discuss his work

14

with interviewers on any really serious level; I have come to admire it. It seems so much in keeping with the character of the films themselves that their creator should be such a delightfully modest and unassuming man who makes no claims for his art outside the evidence of the films. He leaves that to the commentators—it is their job, not his. The attitude can be illustrated with that splendid moment in the interview in *Movie* 6. Hitchcock has been asked to express an opinion on the thematic "broadening out" of his later films: "Well, I think it's natural tendency to be less superficial, that's Truffaut's opinion—he's been examining all these films. And he feels that the American period is much stronger than the English period : . ." He is the least self-conscious of great artists: that delight in creation of which the films themselves speak sufficiently clearly is accompanied by no sense of artistic self-importance. One cannot help thinking again of Shakespeare, content apparently to leave supreme masterpieces to the mercy of producers and actors, not even considering (as far as we know) that perhaps some of them ought to be preserved in print. The delight in creation was its own reward, its own justification.

But when one turns from British to French criticism of Hitchcock one is not made altogether happier. Eric Rohmer and Claude Chabrol deserve our gratitude for their pioneer work: their book on Hitchcock constitutes a very serious attempt to account for the resonances his films can evoke in the mind. One admires its many brilliant perceptions, and the authors' interest in the moral qualities of Hitchcock's films. It leaves one unsatisfied, however: with the feeling that, if that is all Hitchcock offers, the authors over-rate him, and a complementary feeling that, no that is not all he offers. Their analyses—they set out to cover all Hitchcock's films, British and American, up to and including *The Wrong Man,* more than forty films in 150 pages of text—have the effect of depriving the films of flesh and blood, reducing them to theoretical skeletons. And one is always aware, behind the enterprise, of the authors' sense of the need to make Hitchcock seem "respectable". Accordingly, they play down the suspense element and the comedy, and strip each film down to some bald intellectual postulate. The sort of thing I mean is suggested by the remarks Miss Houston quotes in her *Figure in the Carpet*—the work immediately under consideration is *Strangers on a Train*: "One must consider Hitchcock's work in exactly the same way as that of some esoteric painter or poet. If the key to the system is not always in the door, or if the very door itself is cunningly camouflaged, this is no reason for exclaiming that there is nothing inside." This seems to me most misleading. The meaning of a Hitchcock film is not a mysterious esoteric something cunningly concealed beneath a camouflage of "entertainment": it is there in the method, in the progression from shot to shot. A Hitchcock film is an organism, with the whole implied in every detail and every detail related to the whole. In Spenser's words,

"For of the soul the body form doth take;
And soul is form and doth the body make".

If we can't find the "soul" of a work of art expressed in its body, informing and giving life to every limb, then we may be pretty sure it is not worth looking for.

The Rohmer-Chabrol book suffers also from a refusal to look at the films empirically: the authors have decided in advance on their thesis and the films have to be made somehow to fit it: they are Catholic films. Hence the significance of *Rear Window* "is impossible to grasp without a precise reference to Christian dogma". Were this true, the film would surely have to be accounted a failure: a successful work of art must be self-sufficient, its significance arising from the interaction of its parts. But the assertion is of course ridiculous, and it leads Chabrol and Rohmer to distort the film drastically. According to them, for instance, the last shot of the film shows James Stewart and Grace Kelly "in the same state, exactly as if nothing had happened"; yet at the start of the film Stewart was on the point of breaking with Kelly, and at the end they are engaged to be married; and his back is now turned to the window. Again, according to Rohmer and Chabrol, *Rear*

Window offers us a straightforward denunciation of curiosity. A strangely equivocal denunciation, surely, that has most people coming away from the cinema peering fascinatedly through other people's windows. And the curiosity has, after all, brought to light a peculiarly hideous murder and saved a woman from suicide. Hitchcock's morality, with its pervading sense of the inextricability of good and evil, is not so simple.

The articles of Jean Douchet, published in *Cahiers du Cinéma* under the title *La Troisième Clef d'Hitchcock,* seem to me, for all their interpretative excesses and, again, a tendency to reduce things to abstractions, more generally persuasive; especially the accounts, in the last instalment, of *Rear Window* and *Psycho* (*Cahiers du Cinéma* No. 113). Douchet is not in the least embarrassed by Hitchcock's popularity or by his suspense techniques; indeed, these become the starting-point of his analyses. But, again, I feel he oversimplifies, through a fixed determination to pursue one line of approach. To see the flats across the courtyard in *Rear Window* as a sort of cinema screen on which James Stewart "wish-fulfils" his secret desires is splendidly illuminating; but by the end of the argument we seem to have forgotten the fact that the murderer is a real man who has murdered a real woman, deposited real limbs around the country, and buried a real head in a real flower-bed. Douchet's insistence on black magic, initially interesting, seems eventually to limit the significance of Hitchcock's films rather seriously. His treatment of *Psycho,* from the point of view of Hitchcock's control and manipulation of audience-reaction, seems to me—despite disagreements over detail—brilliant, but it covers only one aspect of a complex film. Nevertheless, Douchet's work—and the Rohmer-Chabrol book—are so far beyond anything the British "Establishment" has given us in intelligence and critical rigour that one feels ungrateful in advancing any criticism of them. Even their moments of lunacy seem more intelligent than the relentless triviality of "establishment" reasonableness. The worst harm done by using black magic or "precise reference to Christian dogma" to explain a Hitchcock film lies in the resulting suspicion that the films cannot stand up without such support.

* * *

But, it will be objected, I am not answering my opening question: what can one adduce, positively, once all the false preconceptions have been cleared away, to encourage the doubters to believe that Hitchcock deserves serious consideration as an artist? To answer such a question it will be necessary to advance claims and make assertions that only detailed analysis can justify, and this I shall try to provide in subsequent chapters. Meanwhile I can only ask sceptical readers not to dismiss the assertions before they have given some attention to the attempted justification that follows.

First, then, one might point to the *unity* of Hitchcock's work, and the nature of that unity. I mean of course something much deeper than the fact that he frequently reverts to mystery-thrillers for his material; I also mean something broader and more complex than the fact that certain themes—such as the celebrated "exchange of guilt"—turn up again and again, although that is a part of it. Not only in theme: in style, method, moral attitude, assumptions about the nature of life: Hitchcock's mature films reveal, on inspection, a consistent development, deepening and clarification. Now almost any body of work by a single person will reveal unity of some sort: not only the oeuvre of an Ian Fleming, but of an Agatha Christie and even an Enid Blyton. But this steady development and deepening seems to me the mark of an important artist—essentially, that which distinguishes the significant from the worthless. There is discernible throughout Hitchcock's career an acceleration of the process of development right up to the present day, when the rate is such that the critic can perhaps be forgiven if it sometimes takes him a little time to catch up.

But within this unity—and this is something which rarely receives the emphasis it deserves—another mark of

Hitchcock's stature is the amazing *variety* of his work. No need to point to the obviously "different" films like *Under Capricorn:* consider merely Hitchcock's last five films, made within a period of seven years, *Vertigo, North by Northwest, Psycho, The Birds, Marnie*. There are plenty of points of contact: the use of identification techniques to restrict the spectator, for a time, to sharing the experiences of a single consciousness, in *Vertigo* and *Psycho;* the birds in *Psycho* and *The Birds;* the theme of the parent-child relationship in *Psycho* and *Marnie;* the "therapeutic" theme in all five films (common to almost all Hitchcock's mature work). But even more striking is the essentially *different* nature of each work, in tone, style, subject-matter, method: though one is constantly aware that all five are manifestations of a single genius, there is no repetition; each film demands a different approach from the spectator.

The thematic material of Hitchcock's films is much richer than is commonly recognized. True, he never invents his own plots, but adapts the work of others: again, one cannot resist invoking Shakespeare. Hitchcock is no more limited by his sources than Shakespeare was by his. The process whereby Greene's romance *Pandosto* was transferred into the great poetic drama of *The Winter's Tale* is not unlike that whereby Boileau and Narcejac's *D'Entre les Morts* became *Vertigo:* there is the same kind of relationship. Shakespeare found it necessary to make no greater changes in Greene's plot than did Hitchcock in Boileau and Narcejac's; the transmutation takes place through the poetry in Shakespeare and the *mise-en-scène* in Hitchcock. Nor is this a matter of mere decoration: Shakespeare's poetry is not an *adornment* for Greene's plot, but a true medium, a means of absorbing that plot into an organic dramatic-poetic structure; precisely the same is true of Hitchcock's *mise-en-scène* in *Vertigo*. Naturally, this transmutation of material does not always take place so successfully, without leaving intractable elements: Shakespeare has his *Cymbeline,* Hitchcock his *Spellbound*. In such cases, the artist tends to return later to a richer, more organic treatment of material which is closely related but from which the intractable elements are absent: thus Shakespeare writes *The Winter's Tale,* and Hitchcock makes (though this somewhat exaggerates the relationship to the earlier work) *Marnie.*

The mystery-thriller element is, in fact, never central in Hitchcock's best films; which is not to deny its importance. We could put it this way: "suspense" belongs more to the method of the films than to their themes (in so far as any distinction is possible, such distinctions applied to organic works being necessarily artificial). Look carefully at almost any recent Hitchcock film and you will see that its core, the axis around which it is constructed, is invariably a man-woman relationship: it is never a matter of some arbitrary "love-interest", but of essential subject-matter. This will be readily granted, one supposes, of *Notorious, Vertigo,* or *Marnie;* but it is equally true of *Rear Window* and *North by Northwest.* Of the obvious exceptions, *Psycho* derives most of its power from its sexual implications and overtones—from the impossibility, for Norman Bates, of a normal sexual relationship—and *Rope* much of its fascination from the equivocal relationship between the two murderers (the whole action can be seen as a working-out of suppressed homosexual tensions). Of other partial exceptions, *Strangers on a Train* would be more completely satisfying were its central love-relationship more fully realised; and the failure of *I Confess* seems due in part to the fact that the protagonist is a priest—the most interesting sequences are those dealing with his past love-affair.

It is true that one can find a profound theme underlying almost anything if one is predisposed to search it out sufficiently diligently; what distinguishes a work of art is that this theme should be seen, on reflection, to inform the whole—not only the "content" (if there is such a thing as distinct from treatment; for what is the content of a film but sounds and images, and where else can we look for its style?), but the method. Think seriously about *Vertigo* and *Psycho,* and you will find themes of profound and universal significance; think again, and you

20

will find these themes expressed in the form and style of the film as much as in any extractable "content". The subject-matter of Hitchcock's *Vertigo* (as distinct from Boileau and Narcejac's) is no longer a matter of mere mystery-thriller trickery: it has close affinities with, on the one hand, Mizoguchi's *Ugetsu Monogatari,* and on the other, Keats's *Lamia.* To adduce these generally respected works is not to try to render *Vertigo* respectable by means of them—there is no sleight-of-hand involved of the "A is like B so A is as good as B" variety. *Vertigo* needs no such dishonest apologia, having nothing to fear from comparison with either work (it seems to me, in maturity and depth of understanding as in formal perfection, decidedly superior to Keats's poem if not to Mizoguchi's film). I want merely to ensure that the reader considers Hitchcock's film, not the plot on which it is based; the merits and demerits of Boileau and Narcejac are as irrelevant to *Vertigo* as are those of Greene to *The Winter's Tale.*

More practically, perhaps, in answer to my opening question, one can point to the disturbing quality of so many Hitchcock films. It is one of the functions of art to disturb: to penetrate and undermine our complacencies and set notions, and bring about a consequent readjustment in our attitude to life. Many refer to this quality in Hitchcock but few try to account for it: how often has one heard that a certain film is "very clever" but "leaves a nasty taste in the mouth" *(Shadow of a Doubt, Rope, Strangers on a Train, Rear Window . . .)*: This "nasty taste" phenomenon has, I believe, two main causes. One is Hitchcock's complex and disconcerting moral sense, in which good and evil are seen to be so interwoven as to be virtually inseparable, and which insists on the existence of evil impulses in all of us. The other is his ability to make us aware, perhaps not quite at a conscious level (it depends on the spectator), of the impurity of our own desires. The two usually operate, of course, in conjunction.

This disturbing quality is frequently associated with the Hitchcockian "suspense", and it is this which I would like to consider next. It is very rarely a simple thing, very rarely "mere" suspense; but it is not easy to define, since it has many functions and takes many forms. Jean Douchet's definition—"the suspension of a soul caught between two occult forces, Darkness and Light"—although one of those phrases that sounds better in French than in English, strikes me as too abstract and generalised to be much help. Starting with something concrete, let us attempt two obvious but illuminating exercises in "practical criticism".

Compare, first, the crop-dusting sequence in *North by Northwest* with the helicopter attack in *From Russia With Love* (there is a fairly clear relationship between the two). The difference in quality will seem to some readers too great and too obvious for the comparison to be worth making; but its purpose is not to score easily off a bad film but to help us define the quality of the suspense in Hitchcock. It is worth, perhaps, pointing out that *From Russia With Love* represents precisely that pandering to a debased popular taste that Hitchcock is widely supposed to be guilty of; the most hostile commentator would find difficulty in paralleling its abuses of sex and violence in any Hitchcock film. The film itself, in fact, need scarcely detain us: it will be generally agreed that the sole *raison d'être* of the helicopter sequence is to provide a few easy thrills. From a purely technical viewpoint (if such a thing exists) the Hitchcock sequence is clearly incomparably superior: it is prepared with so much more finesse, shot with so much more care, every shot perfectly judged in relation to the build-up of the sequence. Delicacy and precision are themselves strong positive qualities. In comparison, the Bond sequence is messy and unorganised, the *mise-en-scène* purely opportunistic. But there is far more in question here than the ability to construct a "suspense" sequence: the suspense itself in *North by Northwest* is of a different order. The suspense in the Bond sequence is meaningless: the attack is just an attack, it has no place in any significant development, there is no reason apart from plot—no *thematic* reason—for it to happen to Bond then or to happen in the way it does; it has no effect on his character. The suspense consists solely of the question:

22

Will he get killed or not? and as (a) we know he won't and (b) there seems no possible reason to care if he does, it has no effect beyond a purely physical titillation. In *North by Northwest* the crop-dusting sequence has essential relevance to the film's development. The complacent, self-confident Cary Grant character is shown here exposed in open country, away from the false security of office and cocktail-bar, exposed to the menacing and the unpredictable. The man who behaved earlier as if nobody mattered except himself, is here reduced to running for his life, scurrying for cover like a terrified rabbit; he is reminded —and we, who found him smart and attractive in his accustomed milieu, are reminded—of his personal insignificance in a vast, potentially inimical universe. The sequence marks a crucial stage in the evolution of the character and his relationships, and through that, of the themes of the whole film. If the character were not attractive, for all his shortcomings, our response would be merely sadistic, we would delight in the spectacle of an unpleasant man getting his deserts; but we have become sufficiently identified with him for our suspense to be characterized by a tension between conflicting reactions to his predicament.

North by Northwest is not, however, one of the Hitchcock films that evokes a really disturbing or complex response. The instance I have given, however stunning, shows Hitchcock's suspense at its simplest (in the context, that is, of his recent work). A second comparison will take us a stage further, and once again I shall choose a film that bears a clear relationship to Hitchcock's work: Robert Aldrich's *Whatever Happened to Baby Jane?*, made a few years after the great box-office success of *Psycho*. The comparison is the more interesting in that Aldrich's film has its defenders, and Aldrich himself some intellectual pretensions. Consider the sequence in which Joan Crawford, the crippled sister, struggles downstairs to telephone for help while Bette Davis, who is victimizing, perhaps killing her, is on her way back to the house from town. One is aware here primarily of a sense of great effort

23

which is not entirely explicable in terms of an attempt to convey the agony of the crippled woman's rung-by-rung descent. Indeed, if almost nothing in the film works, it certainly is not for want of trying: every incident is milked for every drop it can yield and more, so that one often becomes embarrassedly aware of Mr. Aldrich tugging determinedly at a dry udder. But what is the purpose of this particular suspense sequence? To arouse our pity for a helpless woman? But it is totally unnecessary to go to these lengths to do that; so we cannot help suspecting that we are rather being asked to relish her suffering. The suspense seems to me entirely gratuitous, in fact. It carries no implications beyond "Will she or won't she?"; no overtones or resonances. The cross-cutting between the sisters has no purpose beyond prolonging the agony. Since Bette Davis is unaware of what is happening, there is no complementary struggle on her side and the moment of her return is entirely fortuitous. In any case, the film's trick ending, in the manner of *Les Diaboliques,* makes nonsense of everything that has gone before.

Compare, first, the cross-cutting between the tennis-match and the murderer's journey to deposit the incriminating lighter in *Strangers on a Train.* The tension generated here has meaning in that it arises from a trial of skill and endurance for both men (the winning of the match, the regaining of the lighter from the drain); all manner of resonances are aroused in the mind (stopping just short, perhaps, of a fully formulated symbolism) by the cross-cutting between the hand straining down into darkness and the struggle for victory in the match in brilliant sunshine; and the most complex reactions are evoked in the spectator, who cannot help responding to the efforts of *both* men. Or compare with the Aldrich sequence the scene in *Rear Window* where Grace Kelly is surprised while searching the murderer's rooms. Our suspense here is inseparable from the suspense of James Stewart, who is responsible for her danger but quite powerless to *do* anything: it is as if *we* had sent her there and must now watch her pay for *our* curiosity. In other words, the sus-

24

pense has that characteristic Hitchcockian *moral* quality, the experiencing of the suspense being an essential factor in the evolution of the James Stewart character and an integral part of its complex meaning.

Instances could be multiplied: the celebrated Albert Hall sequence from *The Man Who Knew Too Much* (1956 version), where the suspense is the outward projection of the agonising conflict within the heroine's mind —Hitchcock's way of making us share that conflict; the descent of the staircase at the end of *Notorious,* where Ingrid Bergman is being rescued from much more than a gang of spies and death by poisoning, and where our response is further complicated by a certain compassion for the Claude Rains character. Enough has perhaps been said to demonstrate the complexity of this concept of "suspense" in Hitchcock's films. I said earlier that it belonged more to his method than to his themes (while denying that any clear-cut distinction between the two was possible). It is sometimes his means of making the spectator share the experiences of the characters; it sometimes arises from a tension in the spectator between conflicting responses; it is sometimes not entirely distinct from a growing discomfort as we are made aware of our own involvement in desires and emotions that are the reverse of admirable. It is one of the means whereby we *participate* in Hitchcock's films rather than merely watch them; but this does not constitute a definition: we must always bear in mind the complex moral implications of the experiences we share or which are communicated to us.

In fact, of the many Hitchcock imitations I have seen, the only one (Ricardo Freda's *Terror of Dr. Hichcock* is in a different category, being less an imitation than a *hommage,* with a highly personal character of its own) that catches something of the true quality of Hitchcockian suspense—and that only for a few moments—is Stanley Donen's *Charade.* I am thinking of the sequence near the end among the pillars outside the Comédie Française where Audrey Hepburn has to choose, in a matter of seconds, between two men who are both demanding her trust, and the suspense is the projection of the conflict within her between instinct and reason—shall she trust the man she loves but whose behaviour has been extremely equivocal, or act rationally and give the treasure she is carrying to the other man? These moments apart, the film is a shallow pastiche.

The theme adumbrated here—the necessity for trust above all, whatever the risks—is the theme of one of Hitchcock's early, and not entirely satisfactory, Hollywood films, *Suspicion*. I pass to this now because it offers a convenient focal point for disentangling two threads which run through Hitchcock's later work and, while they do not in themselves *explain* his films, offer a means of access to them. I had better say that the mystery surrounding the genesis of this film—whether or not Hitchcock reversed the ending at the last moment, and whether, if he did, it was against his own wishes, is irrelevant: we are concerned only with the finished work. Such a last-minute decision might help to explain the slightly "uncooked" quality of much of the film; since its whole significance, as we have it, depends on the ending as it stands, it is difficult to believe that Hitchcock was strongly opposed to it.

First, what I call the *therapeutic* theme, whereby a character is cured of some weakness or obsession by indulging it and living through the consequences. Joan Fontaine falls in love with and marries Cary Grant. He is soon revealed as a liar and she comes to suspect that he is a murderer—eventually, that he is trying to murder *her*. The suspicions poison their marriage, making any open communication between them impossible. Only when they are eventually forced into the open is the fallacy exposed and, in the film's very last shot, a new start is made. Two shots are worth singling out. The first gives us the moment of crystallisation of the suspicions. The couple are playing a word-game with the husband's best friend; as the two men talk, the woman's hands finger the letters on the table, absently arranging them, and suddenly they have formed the word "Murder". Immediately she "realises" that her husband is planning to kill the other man. A

26

marvellous depiction of the way the conscious mind can be guided by the subconscious: in its context, of how deeply entrenched values can manipulate conscious thought. For Joan Fontaine, at the outset, is a dowdy, repressed young woman, a colonel's daughter, who has led a sheltered life characterized by the rigid values of respectability and a total ignorance of the outer world. She is irresistibly attracted to the man who represents glamour and reckless, carefree abandon; but he represents also a total rejection of everything her family background and upbringing has stood for: subconsciously, she *wants* him to be a murderer.

The second shot occurs later in the film, a long-shot where we see Joan Fontaine, now certain that her suspicions are justified, standing in a black dress before a window whose framework casts around her a shadow as of a huge web. She is feeling herself the victim, the fly caught in the trap. But the image suddenly gives us the truth— she is in reality the spider, fattening herself on her suspicions in the centre of the web she has herself spun; or she is both spider and fly at once, victim of her own trap. The image anticipates the even more powerful one in *Psycho* where Norman Bates, sitting in his room beneath stuffed birds of prey, becomes, simultaneously, the bird (from his resemblance to it) and its victim (from his position under it).

The second thread is the extension of this "therapy" to the spectator, by means of encouraging the audience to identify. The outlook of the Joan Fontaine character is a very common one, certainly not restricted to colonels' daughters. From the time of her marriage onwards, we are restricted to the one consciousness: we know only what she knows, see only what she sees: we share her suspicions and learn from experience with her. With her, we find the Cary Grant character attractive: he is so romantic and dashing, so careless of mundane cares and restraints. But with her, we are gradually dismayed by his excesses: the reckless abandon with other people's money—and other people's feelings—comes to appear very unpleasant.

So we become ashamed of having found him so attractive: if he were a complete blackguard, now, we would be exonerated, merely the victims of deceit, and we would be revenged on him when his downfall came. As Joan Fontaine's fingers arrange those letters into the word "Murder", the camera places us in her position: they are *our* hands. The film endorses the man's attitude to life no more than the woman's: if the limitations of her inhibited, sheltered respectability are chastised, so is their inevitable complement—the attraction towards total irresponsibility. And always it is our own impulses that are involved, not only the characters'.

* * *

I have tried in this introduction, to give some rough basis for the analyses of seven films that follow. I decided on Hitchcock's five most recent films for detailed study, first, because they seem to me to constitute an astonishing, unbroken chain of masterpieces and the highest reach of his art to date; secondly, because they offer such variety; thirdly, because they are likely to be revived frequently in coming years, enabling interested readers to submit my analyses to the test of re-seeing the films; finally, because they have received very little serious critical attention in this country. This last consideration, admittedly, would be little help in the matter of selection; but it is worth drawing the reader's attention here to the work on Hitchcock that appeared in early issues of *Movie:* especially V. F. Perkins's article on *Rope (Movie 7)* and Ian Cameron's 2-part analysis of *The Man Who Knew Two Much (Movie 3 and 6)*. I have decided to add discussions of *Strangers on a Train* and *Rear Window* partly because of their intrinsic merit and their importance in relation to Hitchcock's oeuvre as a whole, partly because they are widely known, having been frequently revived. Before this, however, I shall glance cursorily at a few other films. Any attempt at a complete survey is rendered impossible by the unavailability of certain key films—*Shadow of a Doubt* and

Under Capricorn, for example. Comprehensiveness being impossible, I have simply followed whim; the reader is asked to attach particular significance neither to my selection nor to the proportion of space allotted to any given film, which does not necessarily correspond to my evaluation.

* * *

One day, perhaps, we shall re-discover Hitchcock's British films and do them justice; they are so overshadowed by his recent development as to seem, in retrospect, little more than 'prentice work, interesting chiefly because they are Hitchcock's (just as *Two Gentlemen of Verona* is interesting primarily because it is by Shakespeare). One can of course find most of the later themes and methods adumbrated in them; but who wants the leaf-buds when the rose has opened? The notion that the British films are better than, or as good as, or comparable with the later Hollywood ones seems to me not worth discussion. A delightful little comedy-thriller like *The Lady Vanishes* gives us the characteristic Hitchcock tone, in a primitive state, with its interweaving of tension and light humour; *Rich and Strange,* for all its clumsiness and uncertainties of touch—its clearly experimental nature—gives us the characteristic preoccupation with the marriage union. Ralph Thomas's shamelessly plagiaristic remake of *The 39 Steps,* with its intolerably clumsy handling of suspense and cheaply pornographic humour, nicely sets off the technical finesse and moral purity of Hitchcock's original; on the other hand, *North by Northwest,* with its far greater thematic cohesion, shows the limitations of the early film it superficially resembles. There is about these early films a freshness and spontaneity that the far more carefully composed later films lack; the latter, however, are characterized by a creative intensity that makes a preference for the British films analogous to preferring *The Comedy of Errors* to *Macbeth.*

Of the Hollywood films, one might start with the three made for Selznick: *Rebecca, Spellbound* and *The Paradine*

29

Case, both chronologically and in ascending order of satis-factoriness. *Rebecca* (1940) was Hitchcock's first Holly-wood film, an expensive production, and one guesses he didn't have much say in the script. In any case, the film fails either to assimilate or to vomit out the indigestible novelettish ingredients of Daphne du Maurier's book, and it suffers further from Olivier's charmless performance, which finally destroys our sympathy with the heroine, doting on such a boor. But there are rewards: an excellent scene where Olivier and Joan Fontaine, watching the films they took on their honeymoon, quarrel miserably, and we see simultaneously their past happiness and present wretchedness, two stages in a crumbling marriage (though we are perhaps slightly distracted by wondering how a fixed camera without an operator managed a tracking-shot); a "confession" scene that anticipates *Under Capri-corn;* and the best scenes in the film, those built around George Sanders, which arouse something of the character-istic Hitchcockian complexity of response in our simul-taneous attraction and repulsion.

If the more interesting aspects of *Rebecca* suggest a sketch for *Under Capricorn, Spellbound* (1945) strikes us—with its central case-history of traumatic shock—as superficially a sketch for *Marnie;* though it is in its own right more interesting than *Rebecca.* The trouble here is a split in the thematic material. The chief tension is gen-erated by the development of the Ingrid Bergman-Gregory Peck relationship, the growth of mutual trust, the breaking down of barriers and inhibitions on both sides. The final detection of the murderer is arbitrary and not very interest-ing, for all its audience-suicide shot and scarlet flash (camera in murderer's position, hand holding gun fol-lows Bergman to door, then turns gun towards us and Bang! we're all dead), one of the only instances I can think of in Hitchcock of a *pointless* use of identification-technique, since none of us wants to shoot Ingrid Bergman and we feel no connection of any kind with the murderer. One senses the artist playing about with technique for its own sake because he is not much engaged by his

THE PARADINE CASE: during prison visits, barrister Gregory Peck becomes fascinated by his client (Alida Valli), who is accused of murdering her husband.

NOTORIOUS: Alicia (Ingrid Bergman) begins to realise that her husband (Claude Rains) and his mother (Madame Konstantin) are trying to murder her.

material at that point. Nor do the Salvador Dali dream sequences really belong in a Hitchcock film.

Spellbound is perhaps the most interesting of the three Selznick films; *The Paradine Case* (1947), much less adventurous, is more satisfying. It points forward this time to *Vertigo:* the fascination of Alida Valli for Gregory Peck clearly foreshadows that of Kim Novak for James Stewart: the temptation is of the same kind, but it is here given little of the extraordinary universal significance it has in the later film, the conception being inherently more conventional. The film is marred by the mis-casting— against Hitchcock's wishes—of Louis Jourdan. The court- room *dénouement* is masterly, with its complex and adult moral sense: we never cease to feel sympathy for Valli, and our (and Peck's) last sight of her is very haunting.

Lifeboat (1943) proves a far more complex film than I had expected: childhood memory had simplified it into a rather crude anti-Nazi piece in which the survivors in the lifeboat rescue a German, gradually discover that he is irredeemably wicked and treacherous, and batter him to death, with Hitchcock and the whole film solidly behind them; which is far from being so. The Nazi, as played by Walter Slezak, is by no means a stock villain; he bears a close resemblance to the charming devils of certain other Hitchcock films. Charm he certainly has— a seductive charm that in no way mitigates our final verdict on the deeply-embedded doctrines on which he acts, but which keeps also in our minds the sense of the different man he might have been, a sense of his potential human excellence. On the other hand, the other characters, even the good and gentle radio operator and nurse, reveal a latent brutishness when they turn on him and kill him. Certainly there is provocation: the Nazi has murdered the seaman whose leg he earlier amputated: but Hitch- cock's treatment of the scene leaves no doubt as to his response and ours. The killing is characterized by a messy, uncontrolled violence in which we are shocked to see the nurse (especially) participating: a response confirmed by the protest of the only character who holds back from

32

what amounts to mob violence and lynch-law—the Negro. The scene is extremely disturbing because we share the fury of the attackers sufficiently to feel ourselves personally involved in the killing, and are at the same time made to feel ashamed of that involvement. The film conveys the sense that the attackers' primary motivation is a desire for revenge on a man who has made fools of them.

We find in the film that typical Hitchcockian counter-pointing of despair and optimism. The despair—amazing, really, for an American film made in 1943—arises from the sense that the Nazi is the only person who can control the situation, and that his strength is the strength of the Nazi doctrines—the strength of ruthlessness and inhumanity, of complete lack of scruple in achieving an end. And it is a strength that can serve good ends. Joe, the seaman (William Bendix), would certainly have died from his gangrenous leg if the Nazi (a surgeon in civilian life) had not amputated it; and it is clear that no one else has either the ability or the will-power to perform the operation without him. It is made almost unendurably horrible by the implied primitiveness: the shot of the jack-knife held over the flame to be sterilized makes the blood run cold: the Nazi performs it without the slightest loss of composure. We cannot help admiring him, and it becomes very difficult for us, in the course of the film, to retract our admiration: to draw the line between what is admirable and what detestable, since both spring from the same source. The Nazi is dangerous (as so many film Nazis are not) because there is so much to be said for him. Beside him, the morally pure characters are impotent. And it is significant that the character who comes nearest to being a "hero"—the Marxist stoker (John Hodiak)—is the nearest (the point is made explicitly) to the Nazi in outlook, having a similar ruthless determination whose effect is softened however by our awareness that it springs from warm human sympathies. If Hitchcock shows himself, in *Lifeboat* and in *Rope,* a committed anti-Fascist, he does not on the other hand show himself a committed democrat. The alert reader may think ahead to Mark

Rutland in *Marnie;* though it should be insisted that Hitchcock would probably not endorse the translation of Mark's behaviour into political terms: it is made valid only by being rooted in a deep instinctive-sympathetic flow.

The optimism that qualifies this implicit despair is revealed in a variation on the experience-therapy theme. The Tallulah Bankhead character is marvellously realised throughout the film, a very precise, complex attitude to her defined: points for, points against. What we watch, as the film develops, is the gradual stripping away of all the artificial barriers she sets between herself and life— seen primarily in her cynical toughness, partly a pose, partly the manifestation of a real strength—until the real woman emerges. The last stage is reached when her much-vaunted diamond bracelet (she has sworn she will never part with it, and it acquires a symbolic importance, as a trophy, as a means of self-exhibition, as an embodiment of false values) is lost after being used in an attempt to catch fish. Her uncontrollable laughter, we are made to feel, manifests not so much hysteria as a sense of release: she has lost all the external trappings that seemed to compose her identity, and finds that nonetheless she still exists, she is still *there* as a human being. *Lifeboat* may not be mainstream Hitchcock in method—the spectator is left unusually free throughout to regard the action from an objective, detached viewpoint, and there is no clear central figure—but it is central enough in its underlying themes and its complex moral position.

Notorious (1946) is such a rich film that one hesitates to attempt an assessment of its significance in a few lines. I shall content myself with pointing to the sensitivity and insight with which the Grant-Bergman relationship is developed, passing through its phase of mutual destructiveness to become mutually healing, and the complexity of response that arises from its juxtaposition with a second love-relationship, that of Sebastian (Claude Rains) and his mother (Madame Konstantin), many subtly moving effects being achieved through the subsequent modification of the spectator's sympathies and interest. It is perhaps Hitchcock's most fully achieved film to that date. The progress of the relationship is summed up in two love scenes: a progress from the desperate sensuality, betraying the underlying instability, of the lovers' kissing on the balcony near the beginning, to the sure, wondering, protective tenderness of the embrace when Grant at last comes to rescue Bergman from the situation into which he has perversely allowed her—even encouraged her—to be plunged.

Kisses in Hitchcock, one may remark parenthetically, are often used to reveal or epitomise a whole relationship and (if one works outward from that) the sense of a whole film. Consider, besides the present instance, the contrasted relationships between husband and wife, wife and lover, stated simply by cutting from kiss to kiss in *Dial M for Murder;* the stiff embrace, quite lacking in real intimacy, between Farley Granger and Ruth Roman in *Strangers on a Train;* Grace Kelly covering with kisses the unresponsive face of a James Stewart engrossed in his obsession in *Rear Window;* the prolonged and detailed kiss, with 360° camera-track, to convey at once the near-triumph of illusion and the growth of doubt in *Vertigo;* the kiss in *North by Northwest* with Cary Grant's hands encircling Eva Marie Saint's head as if to crush it; the awkward, tentative embrace in the kitchen in *The Birds;* the poignance of the kisses in *Marnie,* with the man's masculine protective tenderness trying to penetrate the woman's frozen unresponsiveness, revealed in huge close-up.

Rope (1948)—apart from its very first shot—takes place entirely within a single apartment and is filmed entirely in ten-minute takes, with an attempt at unbroken continuity not only of time but of *regard.* Some said, absurdly, that it was mere filmed theatre. On the contrary, it is one of the most cinematic of films, carrying one of the defining characteristics of the medium—its ability to use a camera as the eye of the spectator, to take him right into an action, show him round inside it as it were—to its ultimate conclusion. Even were we allowed, however, to go up on the stage and prowl around among the actors, peering into their faces, studying their gestures, their movements, their reactions, this would still not offer a real analogy. For in *Rope,* if we say that the camera becomes the spectator's eye, we must add that it is an eye that sees only what Hitchcock wants it to see, *when* he wants it to see it. The camera, used constantly to link one action or gesture or glance to another in a continuous movement, generates terrific tension, the spectator's eye guided relentlessly to the significant detail at the significant moment. The ten-minute take is one manifestation of Hitchcock's suspense technique. As a piece of virtuosity the film is extraordinary, with timing, in complex actions involving several actors and complicated tracks, that takes the breath away. But technique—suspense itself—is here, as in all the films in which one feels Hitchcock really engaged, the embodiment of moral purpose; or, if "purpose" suggests something too cut-and-dried, a "film with a message", then the vehicle for conveying Hitchcock's complex moral sense.

The main line of development of the film is less the gradual process whereby the murder is brought to light than that whereby the James Stewart character—Rupert—is brought to realise how deeply he is implicated in it; the two processes in fact coincide, and the quality of the suspense depends partly on this duality of development. But the spectator is caught up in this suspense from the start, for we implicate ourselves by wanting—against our better judgment—these two quite unforgivable young murderers to get away with it, and the suspense of *Rope* is basically the tension between this and our conflicting desire that they be brought to justice. There are more ways than one of making an anti-Fascist film (or an anti-anything film). There is the straight denunciation, that generally has the effect of sending the spectator out with a comfortable feeling of being on the right side, his complacency reinforced; or there is Hitchcock's method, which makes us subtly aware that the evil tendencies are there in all of us, a potentiality rooted in human nature against whose upsurging we must be constantly on our guard. I believe that a film like *Rope* (or *Lifeboat;* or *Rear Window*—to make it clear that the argument can be extended far beyond Fascism) is more socially beneficial than a film like Kubrick's *Paths of Glory,* which, stating its subject and its attitude in terms of simple black-and-white, gives us (for all the disturbing force of the execution sequence) the easy satisfaction of telling the Bad People (through the mouth of Kirk Douglas) what we think of them. Hitchcock (in some respects—vide his TV programmes, his trailers, the advertising he either promotes or permits—the least uncompromising of great artists) never compromises on one basic artistic essential: his films never make explicit statements, their "meaning" being conveyed entirely in terms of concrete realisation, entirely dramatised; but even the least alert spectator must go out of *Rope* feeling uneasy and disturbed, because the tensions of the film—for all the marvellous sense of release when the window is at last opened and the shots fired—are never fully resolved. Art, as opposed to propaganda, because of its necessarily inexplicit nature cannot operate directly on the entirely unaware spectator (or reader); yet a film like *Rope,* while giving such a spectator no "message" to take away, cannot fail to bring nearer to the surface of consciousness those feelings which are first subtly encouraged, and then (dramatically, not explicitly) denounced. There is, of course, a very basic artistic principle involved here: to make clear the range of application, one could point out that Jane Austen used much the same method in *Emma.*

Consider one tiny point, which will have to stand as representative of a moral tone and a method diffused through the whole film. We listen to the clever talk of Rupert and his ex-pupil Brandon (John Dall) about the right of the "superior being" to place himself above accepted morality, even to kill. It is all light-hearted, on Rupert's side at least, his manner relaxed and engaging; we respond to his charm and to the outrageousness—the freedom and irresponsibility—of his joking. But under-

ROPE: left, Brandon (John Dall) and Philip (Farley Granger) beside the chest on which the buffet tea is to be served and in which the body of their victim is concealed; right, Rupert (James Stewart) about to confirm a horrifying suspicion.

STAGE FRIGHT: Jonathan (Richard Todd) seen by Kay Walsh leaving the house where a murder has been committed.

lying this amused response we are never allowed to forget what this philosophy, adopted as a code of life, has led to. The camera tracks away from Rupert and Brandon to the right, where Cedric Hardwicke sits in growing uneasiness, and, just as the camera takes him in, turns to look out of the window. We know he is looking to see if his beloved and belated son is coming—the son whose murdered body is in the chest in the middle of the room—and the smile freezes on our faces. The effect is achieved not only through the actor's performance (which is superb) but by means of the camera movement, which links the father's movement with the other men and at the same time integrates it in the entire situation; a cut there would have made the point much too obvious, and dissipated the emotional effect by losing the continuity of gaze. The camera movement makes us respond simultaneously to two incompatible attitudes whose conflict forces us (whether or not on a conscious level) to evaluate them.

Rope has two weaknesses. Hitchcock carries his decision to preserve continuity to the point of trying to cover up inevitable breaks between ten-minute takes by tracking right up to, then out from, something dark. The effect when Rupert blacks out the screen by throwing open the lid of the chest is electrifying; but there are several points where no dramatic purpose is served by our being led right up to, then away from, a character's back: a straightforward cut would have been less distracting. The second weakness is that the spectator wants—and I think needs—to know just how Rupert *did* mean his teaching to be taken.

In *Stage Fright* (1950) one feels the creative impulse at a comparatively low ebb. Hitchcock for once loses his grip on the spectator and about halfway through one realizes that one is not much interested in finding out what is going to happen. The film, however, if highly unsatisfactory considered as a self-sufficient work, is extremely interesting to anyone interested in Hitchcock, since it abounds in ideas relevant to his development. It is a series of variations on a theme common to films as different as

Notorious, Vertigo, and *North by Northwest:* the discrepancy between Appearance and Reality (behind the credits, a safety curtain rises to reveal, not a stage, but real London backgrounds), and their equivocal nature. Running through the film is an extended comparison between two women, both actresses: "corrupt" star Charlotte (Marlene Dietrich) and "innocent" R.A.D.A. student Eve (Jane Wyman). That Corruption emerges on the whole more sympathetically than Innocence is not due *entirely* to the casting. *Acting* is a leading motif: both women act parts continually and habitually, so that there is constant doubt as to the real nature of each. From the start, it is made clear that Eve is not nearly so much in love with Jonathan (Richard Todd), the poor young dupe framed for a murder we see from the flashback in the opening sequence he didn't commit, as she thinks she is: she is in love with the situation, which enables her to make life into a drama with herself as romantic heroine. Charlotte, in fact, the woman who has framed Jonathan, reveals at one point (when her mask of outrageous callousness and cynicism slips for a moment) that, although not emotionally involved with him, she feels for his predicament more genuinely than Eve does. Eve gradually discovers real love for the handsome inspector (Michael Wilding), and there is an interesting scene in a taxi (horribly overplayed by Jane Wyman, however) which begins as conscious, calculated seduction to help Jonathan, the pretence imperceptibly merging into reality so that no one, least of all Eve, is certain where one begins and the other ends. She remarks (about Charlotte), "Who knows what goes on in a woman's mind?—*I* don't know".

But in a sense, Jonathan himself is the central character, and the subject of a potentially fascinating Hitchcockian experiment. The flashback sequence (where he tells Eve how Charlotte has committed the murder and is framing him) is handled (partly through subjective camera-technique, partly because we see everything, inevitably, from the narrator's viewpoint, knowing only what he tells us) in such a way as to make us identify very

40

strongly with Jonathan in his predicament: Jonathan's fate becomes our fate. We watch the film with a certain complacency, knowing that this nice young man will win through somehow; but we are disturbed by our constant uncertainty as to the sincerity of *both* the women with whom his fate rests. Then, at the end of the film, we suddenly learn that Charlotte hasn't framed him at all: he really *is* the murderer: the ground is cut away from under our feet. The flashback was a deliberate lie (and, whatever Rohmer and Chabrol may say, the images lie as well as the words, quite indisputably). Consequently, our response, when Eve (who set out to save Jonathan) indirectly brings about his death-by-safety-curtain, is highly complex: we are still sufficiently Jonathan to find it a betrayal, we are left with a disturbing sense of participating both in his guilt and in his death, cut off from all possible simple attitudes.

Or so, it seems, we would be if *Stage Fright* were the masterpiece that it ought to have been and sounds on paper. In fact, the meanderings of the scenario in the middle stretches of the film, combined with an oddly lethargic *mise-en-scène,* have dissipated our concentration; Jonathan has been lost sight of for so long that identification has been broken: and the script is conventional enough to allow us to reflect, as Eve falls in love with another man, that Jonathan is probably the murderer after all. It is a film more interesting in retrospect than while viewing.

When Chabrol and Truffaut told Hitchcock during an interview that, of all his films (this was before *Vertigo*) they preferred *Under Capricorn* and *I Confess,* he replied, "I find them too serious": a characteristically self-depreciatory response with which, in the case of the later film (the earlier I cannot comment on, it is too long since I saw it) one cannot help agreeing. *I Confess* (1952) is earnest, distinguished, very interesting, and on the whole a failure: it would be, one would have thought, sufficient answer to those who wish to claim Hitchcock as an overt Catholic apologist. If one looks in this film for any genuine response to the Catholic religion, one looks in vain. The

41

"impressive" use of church architecture is an external substitute, uneasily offered, for any effective realisation of the priest's dilemma—for any conveyed sense of what religion, and the confessional law, mean to him: his vocation comes across as just a factor in the data, nothing more. And the moment when he is seen, in high-angled long-shot, walking along a street, with the foreground of the screen occupied by a statue of Christ bearing the cross, is one of the few moments in all Hitchcock's work where the word "pretentious" rises to one's mind. A significance which has no realised dramatic life is being externally stressed.

The film bears a very close relationship to the one that immediately preceded it: *Strangers on a Train*. For once, the earlier work is the better. The priesthood in *I Confess* is to Father Logan what the political world is to Guy Haines, a world of order which offers a legitimate escape from a disordered past. But *Strangers* has the following advantages: (a) Though very important to the plot, the world of politics is not *central* to it: there is no need for Hitchcock to go into Guy's vocation (such as it is) in detail. *I Confess,* on the other hand, is centered upon a point of Catholic church law: the hero's commitment to his beliefs is of fundamental importance. (b) In *Strangers* Hitchcock feels free to suggest that Guy's vocation is in fact suspect, not untainted by a shallow opportunism; in *I Confess,* while failing to convince us of Logan's dedication, he seems unable or unwilling to imply any criticism of it, or to realise Logan's actual attitude clearly in dramatic terms. (c) The conception of Keller, the murderer, though convincing enough, is far more conventional, less detailed, suggestive and complex, than that of Bruno Anthony in *Strangers*. (d) The famous theme of the interchangeability of guilt, of the hero's involvement with the murderer on more levels than that of plot, not entirely satisfactorily confronted in *Strangers,* is shirked even more in *I Confess* (if indeed it can really be said to be there at all). (e) In the world of *Strangers* Hitchcock seems at his ease, in *I Confess* one senses a constant con-

42

straint; where the earlier film has a marvellous combination of tautness and fluency, the later strikes one as laboured. The constraint is clearly not due to theme, or to faulty construction, but to milieu. It may well be that it is the result, not merely of unfamiliarity, but of the lingering, imperfectly assimilated influence of Hitchcock's early Jesuit upbringing. In any case, *I Confess* seems to me to bear the sort of relationship to his work that *The Princess Casamassima* bears to Henry James's. The cost of the somewhat obtrusive "seriousness" to which Hitchcock retrospectively objected is the sacrifice of so much of the characteristic complexity of tone, the "seriousness" here largely precluding the interplay of irony and humour. The general constraint can be localised in some small uncertainties of touch, a failure on the director's part to respond to a *whole* situation. As the murderer's wife dies and begs for Logan's forgiveness, he seems virtually to ignore her; yet one doesn't feel that any criticism of his lack of humanity is implied, nor indeed that Hitchcock is really aware of the implications of the scene. And Anne Baxter's final withdrawal with her husband, leaving the man she loved in a situation of extreme peril, showing neither concern nor interest, is very awkward and indeterminate in aim.

It is the Anne Baxter character, however, that is the most interesting and successful thing in *I Confess,* both in itself and as an anticipation of Annie Hayworth in *The Birds.* The scene on the boat where she admits to Logan that she still loves him generates more tension than any of the scenes involving Keller. The sense we are given in all her scenes of a life wilfully wasted on a self-indulgent clinging to romantic fantasy (one thinks of *Vertigo* as well as of Annie Hayworth here) carries a powerful moral charge. Especially, one can single out the brilliant use of subjective flashback (during her confession scene), both to characterize her and to evoke the necessary moral judgement on the quality of her life. The flashbacks are extremely stylised in a naïvely romantic manner, each stage in her relationship with Logan seen in terms of

I CONFESS: Father Logan (Montgomery Clift) finds Keller (O. E. Hasse) waiting in the church to confess.

THE WRONG MAN: fears of the loss of identity.

sentimental cliché. This is how she sees the past, this is the dream for which she is perversely sacrificing any possible fulfilment in reality; and this romantically gushing girl descending the steps to her waiting lover, to the accompaniment of a sentimental love-song, is her cherished image of herself. The flashbacks are usually laughed at in a superior, knowing way, on the assumption that it is Hitchcock who is being naïve: he is often too sophisticated for the sophisticated. A particularly subtle touch is the visual suggestion contained in the flashbacks that the lovers did in fact commit adultery: we discover later, through Logan's obviously sincere testimony, that they did not, and realise we have been given a beautiful description of wish-fulfilment. *Stage Fright* is not the only Hitchcock film to contain a lying flashback.

The other Hitchcock film with overt religious content is *The Wrong Man* (1956); and it seems to confirm in part the impression of *I Confess,* though it is a far more successful film. Its first half can stand comparison with anything Hitchcock has done. Particularly, one might point out the thematic connection with *The Birds,* a film so different in tone and subject-matter (indeed, they are in some respects at opposite poles, being respectively the most "realistic"—in the narrow sense—and the most fantastic of Hitchcock's recent films): the theme of the precariousness and vulnerability of the little order we can make in our lives. The imprisonment of Henry Fonda becomes more than a case of mistaken identity, through the very intensity of the images: the treatment of his progress, the gradual stripping away of his means of identification, his personal possessions, the reduction of a man depicted from the start as passive, gentle, slightly ineffectual, lacking any strong identity, to the total anonymity with which he is threatened, makes of it a descent into the underworld—into a chaos-world underlying the surface reality where all men are one man, where values cease to exist, where all particularity is merged. For Balestrero, prison becomes a vision of Hell.

The second half of the film fails to maintain this intensity. The change of the focus of interest to Balestrero's wife (Vera Miles), instead of evoking a more complex response, tends to dissipate the spectator's interest. The failure seems to lie in the realisation, in the actual scene-by-scene plotting of the scenario, rather than in the basic conception. We are shown Balestrero, after his preliminary prison experiences, hovering on the brink of breakdown. Yet it is his wife who goes mad, and it is her madness that saves him. By taking away his chief prop, it places the whole burden of holding together the family unit, on the preservation of which the couple's sense of identity depends, on his shoulders. He is forced to discover unknown strengths within himself, and the film associates this with his discovery of God through prayer. Hitchcock attributes the partial failure of the latter half of the film to the fact that working from a factual story limited his freedom to plan the scenario as he wished. A further cause, on internal evidence, seems to be uneasiness with the *dénouement,* with its suggestion of miracle. The crucial scene in the film, if one takes it as essentially a religious work—the scene where Balestrero's mother exhorts him to pray for help—is, significantly, as laboured and conventional in execution as in writing. It will be recognised that a very delicate problem of belief is involved here. I must confess that I find the same kind of unsatisfactoriness in certain other Catholic works, for example in Hopkins's poem *That Nature is a Heraclitean Fire and of the Comfort of the Resurrection.* Hopkins's treatment of "nature's bonfire" is magnificent in the vitality of its imagery; in his treatment of the resurrection theme the imagery abruptly weakens, becomes unrealised, rather banal, even glib. Similarly, Hitchcock's response to the undermining of a precarious order in the first half of *The Wrong Man* seems so much stronger than his response to the idea of *religious* salvation in the latter. One could perhaps argue that the flaw in both works is caused by the essential incommunicability of the unknowable; it *looks* more like a lack of real conviction, a desire to believe rather than belief itself.

In the final sequences, Hitchcock finds his form again. The confrontation of "Wrong" and "Right" men, where Fonda, by his firm stare at the real criminal, proclaims his preservation, indeed the definition, of the identity that was in danger of being submerged, has great force, and the final scene with the wife in the mental home takes us right into the world of *The Birds*. That Hitchcock's Catholic background has relevance to the assumptions about the universe that underlie his films I would not deny; but it seems to me an indirect relevance. The notion that his cinema is the vehicle for a committed Catholicism is made more than dubious by close inspection of the film which seems, superficially, to endorse it most of all.

2. Strangers on a Train

THE FIRST SHOTS introduce us to two pairs of men's feet as their owners arrive at a station. The two are characterized by means of their shoes: first, showy, vulgar, brown-and-white brogues, second, plain unadorned walking shoes. A parallel is at once established in visual terms: or, more precisely, a parallel is imposed by the editing on what would otherwise be pure contrast. Each shot of the first pair of feet is promptly balanced by a similar shot of the second. On the train, we are shown the feet again, moving to the same table. It is always Bruno's feet that we see first—he arrives at the station first, he sits down first, it is Guy's foot that knocks his accidentally, under the table, leading directly to their getting into conversation. Thus Hitchcock makes it clear that Bruno has not engineered the meeting, despite the fact that he knows all about Guy ("Ask me anything, I know the answers") and has the plan for exchanging murders ready to hand: it is rather as if he is waiting for a chance meeting he knew would come. This gives us, from the outset, the sense of some not quite natural, not quite explicable link between the two men.

The contrast between them is developed explicitly in the dialogue. Guy is planning a career in politics: in Hitchcock's films, politics, government, democratic symbolism (the Statue of Liberty in *Saboteur,* the Capitol in this film, Mount Rushmore in *North by Northwest*), are always associated with the idea of an ordered life, set against potential chaos. Bruno, on the other hand, has been expelled from three colleges for drinking and gambling, and lives mostly for kicks. Guy wants to marry Ann Morton, a senator's daughter; Bruno is associated with his mother (by means of the ornate tie-pin, a gift from her, which bears his name). Bruno, despite the fact that he has flown in a jet and driven a car blindfold at 150 mph, and has a theory that "you should do everything before you die", envies Guy: "I certainly admire people who do things"; and, "It must be pretty exciting, being so important—me, I never do anything important". We register this sense of impotence as probably, at bottom, sexual: it links up with Bruno's voyeuristic prying into Guy's love-life.

Yet behind the contrast, the parallel established by the editing of the opening shots becomes manifest. Both men, like so many of Hitchcock's protagonists, are insecure and uncertain of their identity. Guy is suspended between tennis and politics, between his tramp wife and his senator's daughter, and Bruno is seeking desperately to establish an identity through violent, outré actions and flamboyance (shoes, lobster-patterned tie, name proclaimed to the world on his tie-pin). His professed admiration for Guy is balanced by Guy's increasing, if reluctant and in part ironically amused, admiration for him. Certainly, Guy responds to Bruno—we see it in his face, at once amused and tense. To the man committed to a career in politics, Bruno represents a tempting overthrow of all responsibility. Guy fails to repudiate Bruno's suggestive statements about Miriam ("What is a life or two, Guy? Some people are better off dead") with

STRANGERS ON A TRAIN: top, Guy (Farley Granger) and Miriam (Laura Elliott) argue in the record shop about the divorce; left, Bruno (Robert Walker) examines Guy's lighter; and bottom, Bruno and his mother (Marion Lorne).

any force or conviction. When Bruno openly suggests that he would like to kill his wife, he merely grins and says, "That's a morbid thought"; but we sense the tension that underlies it. When he leaves the train he is still laughing at Bruno; but he leaves his lighter behind. This lighter, on which our attention has already been focussed by a close-up and some commentary in the dialogue, is to be of crucial importance in the plot. It was given to Guy by Ann Morton, and bears the inscription "A to G" with two crossed tennis racquets: it is through his tennis that Guy's entry into politics has become possible. Guy's forgetfulness at this moment belies his dismissive joking air when Bruno asks if he agrees to the exchange of murders ("Of course I agree—I agree with *all* your theories"). He is leaving in Bruno's keeping his link with Ann, his possibility of climbing into the ordered existence to which he aspires. The leaving of the lighter is one of the visual equivalents Hitchcock finds for the interior, psychological analysis of the Patricia Highsmith novel that was his source.

Guy, then, in a sense connives at the murder of his wife, and the enigmatic link between him and Bruno becomes clear. Bruno is certainly a character in his own right, realised in detail with marvellous precision; but he also represents the destructive, subversive urges that exist, though suppressed, in everybody: he is an extension, an embodiment, of desires already existing in Guy. In their first conversation, as they face each other, the cross-cutting between them gives us Guy's face unshadowed, Bruno's crossed with lines of shadow like the shadow of bars. He is continually, in these early stages of the film, associated with shadows and with darkness; the development of the film can partly be seen in terms of his forcing himself into the light for recognition. He understands Guy's darker motives better than Guy does himself: "Marrying the boss's daughter—the short cut to a career": nothing later in the film, and especially not the uneasy, formal relationship between the lovers, contradicts this assessment.

50

The next sequence introduces us to Miriam and defines Guy's position more clearly. Miriam—hard, mean, slovenly, at once contemptible and pathetic in her limitations—is one of those Hitchcock characters created in the round with the utmost economy in a few seconds: a gesture of the hands, a drooping of the mouth, a slovenly way of turning the body, dull yet calculating eyes peering shortsightedly through those spectacles. She is more than a character. We are introduced to her in the record shop where she works, and the association of her with revolving objects (taken up later in the fairground sequence) suggests the futile vicious circle of her existence, the circle from which Guy wishes to break free. We have already seen Guy's lack of insight into other people in his inability to deal firmly with Bruno, and seen too that this lack is basically one of self-awareness; so we have no difficulty in accepting the premise of his involvement with Miriam.

After the row in the record shop, during which Guy "warns" Miriam and shakes her violently, the phone call to Ann: "You sound so savage, Guy"—"I'd like to break her foul, useless little neck . . . I said I could strangle her"—shouted over the roar of an approaching train. Cut to Bruno's hands—his mother has just manicured them, and he is admiring them, flexing the fingers. The cut finally clinches the relationship between the two men, making Bruno an agent for the execution of Guy's desires.

The fairground and amusement park is a symbolic projection of Miriam's world: a world of disorder, of the pursuit of fun and cheap glamour as the aim of life, of futility represented by the circular motion of roundabout and Great Wheel that receive such strong visual emphasis in almost every shot. The whole sequence is realised with a marvellous particularity and complexity. Through Miriam, Hitchcock evokes a whole social milieu, small town life in all its unimaginativeness and restriction. The sequence is introduced by the long-shot of Miriam's home, from Bruno's viewpoint, as he waits for her to emerge: respectable-looking, white-fronted house, mother sitting outside on porch, calling, "Now don't be out late" to Miriam as she runs down the steps with her two boy-friends, holding hands, giggling childishly. We think back to the sullen girl in the record shop. At the fairground, she makes the boys buy her an ice-cream cornet, talking at the same time about hot dogs, and they tease her about eating so much. We remember that she is pregnant. She talks about her "craving"—the boys laugh: "Craving for what?" She turns, gazing round the fairground through her spectacles, licking at her ice-cream like a spoilt school-girl, looking at once childish and sensual, and her eyes fix on Bruno, watching her from a distance. Not only is the character rendered with precision: an attitude to her is precisely defined, an attitude totally devoid of senti-mentality, astringent yet not without pity. She is not pathetic in herself—she is never aware of needing any-one's compassion—but her situation, the narrow, circum-scribed outlook, the total lack of awareness, is both pathetic and horrible. And what is being defined, ultimately, is the world from which Guy is struggling to escape: contaminated by that world (remember the im-purity, exposed by Bruno, of his motives for wanting to marry Ann), he cannot free himself cleanly as he wants.

The sequence of events leading up to the murder throws further light on both Miriam and Bruno: the strangling is invested with a clear sexual significance. Miriam, at her first glimpse of Bruno, sees something more intriguing—more *dangerous*—than she can find in her two very unmysterious boys. She gives him the "come-on", un-mistakably, demanding to go to the Tunnel of Love loudly, so that he will hear. As her boys fail to ring the bell at the "Test Your Strength" machine, she looks round for him, and when he materialises mysteriously on her other side, she smiles at him. He shows off his strength to her ("He's broken it!"), first proudly flexing his hands, which are emphasized by the low camera-angle, afterwards waggling his eyebrows at her. Then the round-about: circling motion, raucous music, painted, prancing horses, more flirtation from Miriam. She calls—loudly again, like an announcement—for a boat ride. More revolving in the backgrounds as they get the boats: the Big Wheel behind Bruno, huge water-wheel beside the Tunnel of Love ahead of Miriam. From here, the sexual symbolism accumulates strikingly. They pass through an archway to the boats, above which is written "Magic Isle"—where Miriam will shortly be murdered; the boats cross the lake, enter the tunnel (where Bruno's shadow ominously overtakes Miriam's), out again on to the lake. Miriam runs away on the isle, purposely losing the boys. Then a lighter is thrust before her face and struck: "A to G": "Is your name Miriam?" "Why, yes", She smiles seductively, and Bruno drops the lighter and strangles her.

Her glasses fall off, one lens shatters, and the murder is shown to us reflected in the other lens, inverted and distorted. The lens itself recalls lake and tunnel and is a further sexual symbol. The shot is one of the cinema's most powerful images of perverted sexuality, the murder a sexual culmination for both killer and victim. It ends with Bruno's hands enormous in the lens as he moves back from the body. We see the lighter, "A to G", on the grass, and remember Guy's words on the phone: "I could strangle her". Having retrieved it, Bruno returns to his boat through a chaos of promiscuity—pairs of lovers on the grass all round: the chaos world has been finally defined, the "Magic Isle" becomes an island of lost souls. The association of sexual perversion with the sense of damnation will be taken up again more forcefully in *Psycho*. Bruno, with his close relationship with a crazy mother, is an obvious forerunner of Norman Bates.

As he leaves the fairground, Bruno helps a blind man across the road. At the time, it seems merely a cleverly ironic touch, a trifle glib; but in retrospect it takes on a deeper meaning. Henceforth Bruno will be haunted by the memory of Miriam's eyes looking at him through her spectacles in which the lighter-flame is reflected; his helping of a blind man with dark glasses is an act of unconscious atonement. The sequence ends with Bruno looking at his watch: cut to Guy, on a train, looking at *his:* the visual link again used to enforce the connection between them.

Later, we see Guy reaching his rooms in Washington. On one side of the street, stately, respectable houses; towering in the background, on the right of the screen, the floodlit dome of the Senate House, the life to which Guy aspires, the world of light and order. On the other side of the street, deep shadow and tall iron-barred gates from behind which Bruno calls. The light-and-darkness symbolism—Guy turning from the lighted doorway of the house towards the shadow, away from the Senate House —is simple, but not naïve or ridiculous, and handled naturally and unobtrusively. Bruno beckons, a shadow among shadows. Again we see him with bars across his face: at the start of the ensuing dialogue he is behind the bars, Guy in the open. He gives Guy the spectacles, reminds him about the lighter—"I went back for it, Guy". Guy is horrified. Then: "But, Guy, you *wanted* it . . . We planned it together . . . You're just as much in it as I am . . . You're a free man now". The 'phone rings in Guy's rooms, a police car approaches, stops outside, and Guy promptly joins Bruno behind the bars, in shadow: a free man. He says, "You've got me acting like I'm a criminal", and we have a subjective shot of the police from Guy's position behind the bars. The scene gives a beautifully exact symbolic expression to Guy's relationship to Bruno and what he stands for.

More light-and-darkness in the next sequence: Guy answers his 'phone, Ann tells him to come round. Right of screen: a large, lighted lamp, Guy holding the receiver to his ear, Ann's voice coming through. Left of screen: heavy shadow, Miriam's spectacles dangling downwards in Guy's other hand. The hands remind us of a pair of scales. We then see Guy and Ann together for the first time, and Hitchcock shows us their rather remote, uneasy relationship. Ann strikes us as the older, certainly the maturer, the more completed: the dominant partner. Their kiss lacks real intimacy or tenderness. She tells him she loves him and he replies, "Brazen woman, I'm the

54

one to say that": an odd, endistancing, defensive kind of joke. As Ann, her father, and her sister Barbara break the news, and Guy makes a feeble attempt at surprise, our view of the lovers' relationship is confirmed by Ann's obvious suspicions that Guy has killed Miriam: she tells him, with heavy significance, "She was strangled"; and she is visibly relieved when he explains his alibi. If the world from which Guy wishes to escape is defined for us by Miriam, then Ann—formal, rather hard, rather cold, in Ruth Roman's unsympathetic performance—defines the life to which he aspires: a life of imposed, slightly artificial orderliness. As for his guilt, Hitchcock makes it very clear that what he can't bear is, not the idea that he has been indirectly involved, at any rate by desire, in the death of a human being, but the fear of being found out: it is the only feeling he reveals in his conversation with Bruno, and all that he and Ann reveal in this scene. The moral point is made clearly when Senator Morton rebukes Barbara for saying, of Miriam, "She was a tramp," with the remark, "She was a human being". The rebuke, for the audience, has relevance to the lovers as well.

Yet, despite the critical attitude adopted towards the lovers' relationship, we are made aware of its importance for Guy. Ann is more than a way to a career, she represents in herself something of the ordered world he aspires to. Thus the kiss that closes the sequence, which Guy, eyes looking straight into the camera, scarcely returns, is in contrast to the kiss that opened it: the *potentialities* of the relationship are threatened by the concealment of his involvement in Miriam's murder.

In the ensuing sequences Bruno increases the pressure on Guy to murder his father. First, the 'phone call to Ann's house: Guy hangs up. Second, the scene where Guy and Hennessy (the detective detailed to watch him) walk together past the Senate House. In the setting of spacious, ordered architecture, Guy says, "When I'm through with tennis I'm going into politics", and looks across to see Bruno watching from the steps, tiny in long-shot. Third, the letter from Bruno pushed under

Guy's door. Fourth, the scene where Ann sees Bruno for the first time. She and Guy are in the Senate House when Bruno calls Guy from among the pillars: "You're spoiling everything . . . You're making me come out into the open". Fifth, Guy receives the plan of, and key to, Mr. Anthony's house. Then, at last, the famous shot of Bruno watching Guy at the tennis court, all other heads turning to follow the ball, Bruno's conspicuous because motionless, his eyes fixed on Guy: a moment at once funny and unnerving. He now manages to meet Ann while Guy practises.

These scenes work beautifully in terms of suspense, but here as elsewhere it is necessary to ask, of what exactly does this suspense consist? We feel uneasy not just because pressure is being brought to bear on Guy to make him commit a murder; rather, it is because that which he wants to hide is indeed "coming out into the open". Think back to a character I have hitherto neglected: Ann's sister Barbara. In the first scene at Senator Morton's house, Barbara's function is clearly to express, directly and unhypocritically, what everyone—including the spectator—is slightly ashamed to find himself think-ing: that it is really an admirable thing from all points of view that Miriam is dead. Her frank and shocking remarks recall Bruno's justification of killing—"Some people are better off dead"—and therefore involve the spectator with Bruno; they also prompt the senator's re-buke—"She was a human being". In other words, con-flicting, apparently mutually exclusive responses are set up in the spectator, with disturbing results. We respond strongly to Barbara's no-nonsense honesty, but we are made ashamed of that response. It is this conflict within the spectator that is the essence of the ensuing suspense: we, as well as Guy, are implicated in Miriam's murder. Bruno's symbolic progress, each step bringing him closer and clearer—telephone, distant figure, closer figure lurking among shadowy pillars, figure sitting in full sunlight, young man in conversation with Ann, intruder from the chaos-world into the world of order—represents the

STRANGERS ON A TRAIN: the "murder" of Mrs. Cun-ningham. Patricia Hitchcock and the spectator are about to be punished for conniving at the release of destructive forces.

emergence of all we want concealed: our own suppressed, evil desires.

Bruno's appearance at the party marks his final eruption into the world of order: the demand for recognition of the universality of guilt by a world that rejects such an assumption. The centre-piece of the scene—in some respects of the whole film—is Bruno's near-strangling of Mrs. Cunningham. It derives its disturbing power again from a subtly aroused conflict, the attractiveness and danger of that connivance at common guilt which Bruno represents. First, we are disarmed by Bruno's casually irreverent deflation of a dignified, self-righteous judge: how is he able to sit down to dinner after sentencing someone to death? The way the judge responds to the insolent question plainly makes the point that his way of life depends on such questions never being asked. The lightly humorous treatment releases us from some of the uneasiness we feel at responding to Bruno and prepares us for the next step—Bruno's conversation about murder with Mrs. Cunningham.

Here the underlying assumption of the film (subversive, destructive desires exist in all of us, waiting for a momentary relaxing of our vigilance) becomes explicit. Mrs. Cunningham's denial that *everyone* is interested in murder breaks down abruptly when Bruno asks if there haven't been times when she has wanted to kill someone—*Mr.* Cunningham, perhaps? There follows the richly comic exchange of murder methods, culminating in Bruno's demonstration of silent strangling—the method he used on Miriam—with Mrs. Cunningham as guinea-pig. As his hands close on the old woman's throat, Barbara comes up behind her, Bruno sees her and, for the second time, is reminded by her (dark hair, round face, glasses) of Miriam. He goes into a "sort of trance", Mrs. Cunningham is nearly killed, and the sequence ends with Barbara, who has realised that Bruno was really strangling *her,* in tears. The scene is a superb example of the Hitchcock spectator-trap. First, belief in established order has been undermined in the deflation of the judge; then the dia-

58

logue with Mrs. Cunningham and her friend, because of its light tone, gives us licence to accept the notion of common guilt as something of a joke, to connive at it, allowing ourselves to be implicated in the "game" of murdering Mrs. Cunningham, who is anyway a rich, trivial, stupid old woman. Then abruptly the joke rebounds on us: we have nearly been implicated in another murder: swift modulation of tone has seldom been used to such disturbing effect. We are horrified to find that we have momentarily identified ourselves with Bruno (the sequence contains a number of subjective shots, where we are placed in his position). We have the feeling, even, that we, through a lack of vigilance, have released these destructive forces by conniving at them. But the final emphasis is on Barbara; and we recall that earlier it was she who was used to make explicit our conventionally suppressed feeling that Miriam's murder was all for the best. She seemed before to give validity to the release of the anarchic forces of desire; now she is punished by the very forces she helped release, and we with her. The scene leads us straight to the essence of Hitchcock: that ordered life depends on the rigorous and *unnatural* suppression of a powerfully seductive under-world of desire: and we see the reason for the stiff formality of the world of order in the film.

The scene is rich in other ways too. The three minor characters, the judge, Mrs. Cunningham, and her friend, are realised with marvellous economy and precision, the realisation being, as always, as much a crystallisation of an attitude towards them as the objective description of character: there is nothing indulgent about the humour with which these representatives of the world of order are presented. The incident also further illuminates Bruno, whose symbolic function in the film is by no means undermined by the fact that he is also a character created in the round. Mrs. Cunningham, like Bruno's mother, is rich, spoilt, foolish and indulgent; he is able to handle her so adroitly because he is used to managing his mother, manipulating her reactions. This is the kind of relationship he can manage, a relationship based entirely on power, wielded through a combination of cunning and insidious, self-insinuating charm—his ability to involve others in his sickness. Finally, the sequence shows the toll his life and actions are taking of him, his thoroughgoing cynicism and complete lack of remorse belied by his obsession with Barbara's (i.e. Miriam's) glasses and neck, the ineradicable memory of that other relationship expressed in the shot of his anguished face as he tries to strangle Mrs. Cunningham. As his hands are pulled away from her throat, he falls back in a swoon.

It is the near-strangling of Mrs. Cunningham that forces the spectator to come to terms with his attitude to subversive desire, and prompts Guy, under pressure from Ann, to divulge the truth to her: without, however, acknowledging any personal guilt, of which he obviously remains quite unaware. He tells Ann, "I'd do his murder, he'd do mine"; to which she responds suggestively, "What do you mean—*your* murder, Guy?" Her first reaction was, "How did you get him to do it?" The removal of doubts between the lovers marks a necessary stage in the action. Their relationship is now on a surer footing, giving Guy the strength to take steps to extricate himself. The next sequence, in which he visits Mr. Anthony's house at night, is a turning-point and a critical crux.

The emphasis is, again, on suspense: in successive shots we see Guy take the gun Bruno has sent him, elude his "tail" by using the fire-escape, and cross the moonlit lawn of the Anthony grounds in long-shot, like a shadow. We don't know at all clearly what he intends to do or what will happen to him. Suspense is built up as he enters the house (using the key Bruno has sent), consults Bruno's map to find the father's room, encounters a snarling mastiff on the stairs, subdues it, finds the room, transfers the gun, hesitating for a moment with it in his hand, from his breast pocket to his side pocket, creeps into the bedroom, approaches the bed, calls in a whisper, "Mr. Anthony . . . I want to speak to you about your son . . . about

Bruno". Then the dark figure on the bed switches on a lamp and reveals himself as Bruno.

At first glance this seems, indeed, to be that "mere" suspense that is all Hitchcock's detractors see in his films: externally applied, rather cheap. And if we assume that Guy knows precisely what he is going to do in Mr. Anthony's house, the criticism in unanswerable. Hitchcock is cheating, basing the suspense on a deliberate misleading of the spectator. There are, however, points which suggest that this is too superficial a reading: that Guy has indeed made up his mind to visit Mr. Anthony, but there remains a possibility, right up to the moment of hesitation outside the bedroom door, that he will change his mind and shoot him. With this in mind, the sequence assumes quite a different aspect.

The first hint comes in fact several scenes earlier, when Guy is talking to Hennessy in his rooms before the party. The camera looks down as Guy opens the top drawer in which Bruno's gun is lying, and we see the two men, with the gun strongly emphasized in the foreground of the screen. Guy has just been telling Hennessy he will have an early night: he is in fact planning to visit the Anthony house. But they are now discussing Hennessy's suspicious colleague, Hammond, and, as we see the gun in the drawer, Hennessy says, "He doesn't trust anybody— not even himself". The whole shot is framed and directed in such a way as to give a particular significance to the remark, linking it with the gun. Then, in the house, we have the moment of hesitation itself. This is either the decisive moment of the scene of a very cheap trick indeed: cheap, because it falsifies a character's behaviour for the sake of producing a shiver—if the gesture doesn't imply uncertainty as to what to do with the gun, then it has no meaning at all. Finally, shortly after the discovery that it is Bruno on the bed, Guy tells him, "You're sick", adding, "I don't know much about those things . . ." It is the nearest to an explicit statement in the film of that lack of self-awareness so plentifully illustrated elsewhere. The "suspense" of the sequence, then, has a point: the spectator's uncertainty as to what Guy is going to do corresponds to the character's own inner uncertainty. And the moment of final decision is the turning-point of the film: henceforward, Bruno is openly *against* Guy, no longer wanting anything but revenge. The conflict has changed levels, and the struggle for self-preservation is the price Guy must pay for his involvement; an involvement partly expiated by the decision taken outside Mr. Anthony's bedroom.

But, this said, it must then be admitted that to raise such doubts is to acknowledge a dissatisfaction with the sequence. Guy's uncertainty is not sufficiently realised, a fault due perhaps to the limitations of Farley Granger as an actor, which led Hitchcock to put more weight on that one gesture with the gun than it can stand. But the criticism is of a misjudgement, a local failure of realisation, not a major lapse in artistic integrity. [—Now, I'm not so sure. The compromise over the hero-figure that fatally flaws *Torn Curtain* offers a close parallel, and one cannot but feel that Hitchcock's uncertainty of handling in the scene of Guy's visit to Bruno's house has its roots in his fears of the effect of so morally dubious a "hero" on box office response. "Major lapse in artistic integrity" is perhaps not too strong a description.—R.W. 1968.]

* * *

Ann's interview with Bruno's mother is the next step in the working out of the situation on its new level, the protagonists now ranged openly against one another. In Mrs. Anthony's insanity we see (as we are to see it later, more extremely, in the amalgam of Norman Bates and his mother at the end of *Psycho)* the ultimate extension of the chaos world. The woman's very existence depends on the complete rejection of all value-judgements, the final denial of responsibility. In fact, "irresponsibility" is the word she uses to excuse Bruno: with a smile of maternal indulgence, a little knowing shake of the head, she says, "Sometimes he's terribly irresponsible". To which

Ann returns a moment later, "He's *responsible* for a woman's death."

The famous cross-cutting between the tennis-match and Bruno's journey with the lighter gives us a very different sort of suspense—simpler, less disturbing than before, as befits this phase of the action. The tension we feel now is not uncomplicated by conflicting responses (who hasn't *wanted* Bruno to reach the lighter?), but the struggle has become clear and simple, the forces of good and evil are now separate and clearly aligned. Despite this, some very interesting points arise.

First, the development of that elementary yet elemental light-darkness symbolism: Guy fights for victory on the brilliantly sunny tennis court as Bruno struggles to reach the lighter which has slipped through a grating down a drain. One doesn't want to reduce the film to simple, pat allegory (Hitchcock resolutely defies any such treatment) but the cutting between sunny open court and shadowy enclosed drain carries powerfully evocative overtones: underlying the whole action of the film, we can see as its basis the struggle for dominance between *superego* and *id*. Secondly, we remember that tennis has been established from the start as Guy's means of access to the ordered world, his ladder from the previous life with Miriam to his projected political career; it is therefore appropriate that his fate should depend now on his ability at tennis. Furthermore, this test is made explicitly one of character, even of character-development. Guy, in his desperation to finish the match in time, has to change his whole manner of playing (as the commentator points out)—he abandons his usual cautious long-term strategy in favour of a "grim and determined" open battling style. His whole career—even the desire to marry Ann—has been a matter of careful strategy: now he is forced to fight openly for what he wants. Thirdly, it is significant that the outcome of the entire film should be made to depend upon the retrieving of the lighter, symbol of Guy's involvement with Bruno, of his placing himself in Bruno's hands. Great emphasis is laid on it—and on the "A to G" inscription

—every time it appears. It is Guy's strongest *concrete* link with the ordered world; now he must re-enter the chaos-world in order to retrieve it, thereby risking final submersion.

The fairground climax gives us the ultimate development of that world in its magnificent symbol of the roundabout that gets out of control. Guy struggles for his life—for more than his life—on the insanely whirling machine beneath the metallic hoofs of hideously grinning and prancing dummy horses: the horses on which Bruno, with Guy's implicit consent (the lighter), set about "seducing" Miriam. Guy is denied the satisfaction—we are denied the release—of a straightforward victory: the roundabout terrifyingly breaks down, Guy is thrown clear, Bruno is crushed under the wreckage. He dies obstinately refusing repentance, and Guy seems involved forever. Then, as he dies, Bruno's hand opens: the lighter is in his palm.

The very last scene of the film (where Guy and Ann move away pointedly from a friendly clergyman on a train) shows us, with light humour, Guy, united with his senator's daughter, resolutely—even somewhat extremely and rigidly!—resisting the possibility of further temptation. The stiff unnaturalness of the couple's behaviour is perfectly logical: Guy's involvement with Bruno has been worked out in action—he has never faced its implications, and his personality remains to the end unintegrated, his identity still potentially unstable, the threat of disorder to be held back only by rigid control.

Strangers on a Train draws together many themes already adumbrated in earlier films, which will be taken further in later ones: the theme of what Conrad calls the "sickening assumption of common guilt" (developed especially in *Psycho);* the theme of the search for identity *(Vertigo);* the theme of the struggle of a personality torn between order and chaos (perhaps the most constant Hitchcock theme); and, in close conjunction with this, the notion of experience-therapy—the hero purged of his weaknesses by indulging them and having to live out the consequences *(Rear Window)*. We find here, too, the characteristic Hitchcock moral tone: the utterly unsentimental and ruthless condemnation of the forces that make for disorder, coupled with a full awareness of their dangerously tempting fascination; a sense of the impurity of motives: does Guy love Ann, or is she merely the way to success? Clearly both: good and evil are inseparably mixed. And, running through the film, there is that Hitchcockian humour which itself represents a moral position: it is the manifestation of his artistic impersonality, of his detached and impersonal attitude to themes which clearly obsess him. Yet the film leaves one unsatisfied (not merely disturbed). The fault may lie partly with the players: Farley Granger, a perfect foil to John Dall in *Rope,* is too slight a personality to carry much moral weight, so that we feel that Guy's propensity for good or evil is too trivial: Ann (Ruth Roman) is a cold, formal woman, so that there is little sense, at the end, that Guy has won through to a worthwhile relationship. There is not enough at stake: his triumph over too slight an evil (in himself) has won him too equivocal a good. Consequently, the effect seems at times two-dimensional, or like watching the working out of a theorem rather than of a human drama, and the film, if not exactly a failure, strikes me as something less than a masterpiece.

One has no qualifications about Robert Walker's Bruno, or about any of the scenes built around him. The film's two classic sequences, in fact, seem to me the first fairground sequence and the scene of the Mortons' party. Here the characteristic Hitchcockian moral tone is felt in all its disturbing complexity.

3. Rear Window

Rear Window is perhaps the first of Hitchcock's films to which the term masterpiece can reasonably be applied; and at the time of writing no copy of the film is available in this country, either for public or private viewing. I mention this unhappy fact by way both of apology and of protest. Apology, because this chapter is necessarily based on three-year-old memory and a few notes scribbled in the cinema: if there are inaccuracies, and if my analysis is here less particularized, the reader's forgiveness is asked, on these grounds.

There seem to be two ways, in general, of looking at *Rear Window:* (a) It constitutes a whole-hearted condemnation of curiosity, prying, voyeurism, *libido sciendi* and *delectatio morosa* (see Rohmer/Chabrol); (b) A corrupt, distasteful film, it shamelessly exploits and encourages curiosity, prying, etc. etc. . . . Neither of these extremes can stand up to a rigorous analysis of the actual film and of the reactions it provokes in the spectator; the fact that the second is much the easier to defend is no doubt what has forced many of the film's admirers into the false position of defending the first. In fact, the morality of the film is far subtler and more profound that either suggests.

The chief objection to the second view is that we are made to feel far too uneasy, in the course of the film, about the morality of prying, to find it really pleasurable: by explicit discussion in the dialogue (Jefferies and Lisa, hence the audience, are "the most frightening ghouls . . . plunged into despair because we find a man *didn't* kill his wife"), by placing Lisa in grave danger, by our discovery that the murderer is as pitiable as monstrous. The chief objection to the first is that the final effects of Jefferies's voyeurism are almost entirely admirable. If he hadn't spied on his neighbours, a murderer would have gone free (and whatever our views on capital punishment, most of us will agree that it is undesirable that a man capable of murdering a helpless, if maddening, woman, cutting her up in little bits and distributing them round the country, should retain his liberty), a woman would have committed suicide, and the hero would have remained in the spiritual deadlock he had reached at the beginning of the film. If I say at once that I regard *Rear Window* as the clearest statement in Hitchcock of what I have called the therapeutic theme, it will be guessed that I attach great importance to this last point.

First, however, I want to consider another aspect of the film: that suggested by Paul Mayersberg in *Movie 3* when he described it as Hitchcock's "testament", and expounded in a somewhat different form by Jean Douchet in the last of his series *La Troisième Clef d'Hitchcock* in *Cahiers du Cinéma* (no. 113). Douchet's interpretation of the film roughly equates Jefferies (James Stewart) with the spectator in the cinema, the flats across the court with the screen: what Jefferies sees is a projection of his own desires. The parallel is, up to a point, rewarding. Jefferies is presented as a man who has never come to terms with himself; his lack of self-knowledge and consequent tendency to lapse into compulsive behaviour makes him an archetypal Hitchcock protagonist. A news photographer, he has frequently courted death; he refuses all commitment, all personal involvement, escaping from responsibilities by pursuing danger and hectic action recklessly. As Lisa (Grace Kelly) says, he is like "a tourist on an endless vacation". Before the film begins, his leg has been smashed and he is restricted to a wheelchair in his apartment: in other words, he is thrown upon himself, all his usual escape-routes cut off. Lisa, who wants to marry him, is becoming very pressing. He, consequently, is trying to break with her: whenever the question of marriage crops up, his leg itches under the plaster, he feels an uncontrollable urge to scratch. Stella, his visiting nurse (Thelma Ritter) tries to make him see the dangers of his condition, his need for self-knowledge: "We've become a race of peeping-toms. People ought to get outside and look in at themselves". Jefferies's only means of escaping from examining his own condition is by spying on other people—the people in the flats across the courtyard. Stella tells him she can "smell trouble right here in this apartment . . . Look out of the window, see things you shouldn't see". He is "like a father": in fact, we realise that his gazing gives him a sense of power over those he watches, but without any accompanying respon-

REAR
WINDOW:
top, Jefferies
(James Stewart)
and Lisa (Grace
Kelly); and
below, "What
Jefferies sees is
a projection of
his own desires."
With Stella
(Thelma Ritter).

sibility. He tells Stella in reply that "there *is* going to be trouble . . . Lisa Freemont": from the first, a clear link is established between his relationship with Lisa and his spying on the neighbours. He watches the occupants of the flats opposite as a means of escape from his problems, just as the average cinemagoer goes to the movies to escape from his; but the people he chooses to watch (the element of choice is made clear: Hitchcock shows us one happy, seemingly united family in whom Jefferies shows no interest whatever: Stella calls him a "window-shopper") all in some way reflect his own problems, so that his problems are worked out through his gradually growing involvement with them. This is very much how a Hitchcock film works on the lowest level—the level, that is, of the least aware spectator. Jefferies regards Lisa as an encumbrance, and their relationship as a threat to his freedom, to his irresponsibility; he sees a man opposite plagued with a nagging, invalid wife. He would like to get rid of Lisa; he deduces (rightly, as it turns out, though the deduction involves a considerable amount of guesswork) that the man has murdered his wife and is disposing of the body.

Jefferies himself (the resemblance to the hero of *Strangers on a Train* will be clear) never becomes conscious of the connection between what he sees and his personal life, though what is in effect a substitute for that consciousness is forced on him when the murderer invades his apartment. Connections with the other tenants are less obvious but still demonstrably there. Each apartment offers a variation on the man-woman relationship or the intolerable loneliness resulting from its absence, and only the one contented couple is passed over and forgotten. The sterile couple who have made a dog their chief object of affection; the newlyweds stifling (metaphorically) behind closed shutters; "Miss Lonelyhearts", forever enacting romantic situations; all can be taken as representing possibilities before Jefferies and Lisa. The difficulties of human relationships, the horror that marriage can be and the comparable horror of frustrated singleness, are much stressed; and the fact that Jefferies morbidly concentrates—while preserving an apparent ironic detachment—on failed relationships and failed lives, taken in conjunction with his recklessness with his own life, reveal to us the essential features of his spiritual condition.

All this offers clear parallels with the spectator watching the screen. We tend to select from a film and stress, quite unconsciously, those aspects that are most relevant to us, to our own problems and our own attitude to life, and ignore or minimise the rest; and we tend to use such identification—again, usually unconsciously—as a means of working out our problems in fantasy form: often, as it proves with Jefferies, a dangerous tendency but sometimes —again, as with Jefferies—a valuable one. There is an obvious point at which the parallel breaks down: Jefferies sees what, within given limits, he chooses to see; the spectator sees what Hitchcock chooses to show him. And this is especially true, it must be emphasized, of a *Hitchcock* film. When watching, let us say, a Preminger movie —*Exodus* or *The Cardinal*—we are left unusually free to select, to reflect upon the action and reach our own decisions; but in late Hitchcock our responses are themselves very carefully controlled and organised. But despite this objection the parallel largely works because we are led from the outset to identify ourselves with Jefferies, to such an extent that the discrepancy between what *he* sees and what *we* see is considerably narrowed: if the whole film is his enactment of a therapeutic experience, it becomes, by extension, a therapeutic experience for the spectator too.

Rear Window is Hitchcock's most uncompromising attempt to imprison us, not only within a limited space, but within a single consciousness. From the beginning of the film to the end, we are enclosed in the protagonist's apartment, leaving it only when he leaves it (precipitately, through the window!). With one brief exception (when Jefferies is asleep, we see Thorvald, the murderer, leave his apartment with a woman), we are allowed to see only what he sees, know only what he knows. The exception is very important, in fact: the woman *could* be Mrs. Thorvald, and this brings home to us the fact that Jefferies *could* be wrong: by making the identification of the spectator with Jefferies's consciousness not *quite* complete, Hitchcock enables us to feel just that small amount of uneasiness necessary for us to question the morality of what he is doing—our own morality since we are spying with him, sharing his fascinated, compulsive "Peeping-Tom-ism". I have already hinted at the other limitation on identification: the fact that, in the course of the film, we become more consciously aware of the nature of Jefferies's involvement with what he watches than he is himself. But these points apart, identification is forced on us to an unprecedented extent, and preserved throughout the film, as it is not in *Vertigo* or *Psycho*.

The difficulty of the Lisa-Jefferies relationship lies in the refusal of either to compromise. The lack of any give-and-take makes it essentially artificial, sterile, incapable of development. Its essence, and its relationship to Jefferies's spying, is given us, with characteristic economy, on Lisa's first entry. We see Jefferies asleep; then a shadow falls over his face: it is Lisa. She bends over him, kisses him tenderly, and he wakes up. Instantly the relationship becomes an act, Lisa is forced into giving a performance: she could be natural only when he was asleep. "Who are you?", Jefferies asks; and at once she moves back from him, then swirls round the room switching on lamps: "Reading from top to bottom: Lisa"—first lamp—"Carol"—second—"Freemont"—third. We watch a woman become a mannequin, or even a magazine illustration: it is all Jefferies can accept. She turns herself into a public performance, a spectacle to be watched from the other side of the footlights. It is a splendid example of the ability of Hitchcock, or a happy conjunction of director and scriptwriter, to find a means of crystallising a whole situation or relationship or idea in a single image, when he is working at full pressure: the difference between this film and most of *Stage Fright,* or much of the

71

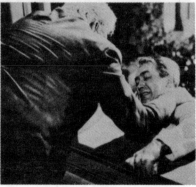

REAR WINDOW: top left,
Thorvald (Raymond Burr);
top right, Thorvald above,
Lisa below; and right, James
Stewart's victory is equivocal.

second half of *The Wrong Man.* Soon, over wine, Lisa tries to "sell" Jefferies a new identity ("I could see you looking very handsome and successful in a dark blue suit") which he resolutely rejects. And of course rightly: the issues in Hitchcock are seldom simple. She goes out to fetch the dinner, and Jefferies immediately turns to spy on the neighbours. He sees first Mrs. Thorvald, the nagging, invalid wife, then "Miss Lonelyhearts", the pathetic spinster, welcoming an imaginary guest, pouring out wine for two. Clearly what he is seeing are two grotesquely distorted images of Lisa: two possible Lisa-identities.

What happens in the Thorvald apartment represents, in an extreme and hideous form, the fulfilment of Jefferies's desire to be rid of Lisa. Because of its extremeness, he reacts against it with horror; and his overcoming of Thorvald (the victory is equivocal) corresponds to the casting out (also, therefore, equivocal) of this desire. Two climactic scenes carry particular significance. The first is where Lisa explores Thorvald's flat and is trapped by him: we watch with Jefferies, sharing his sense of anguish and impotence. It is the turning point in their relationship. He comes to respect her for the courage and initiative (virtues he can appreciate) which he didn't know she possessed (and she does it, obviously, to demonstrate these to him, to make him *see,* not from any abstract desire for justice). But more than that, and simultaneously with it, his desire to be rid of her is abruptly given a form so direct as to be unacceptable: dream has become nightmare. It is this, as much as his new respect for Lisa's pluck, that brings about a recoil in him, allowing the deeper but suppressed need for a permanent relationship to rise to the surface.

In the second climactic scene, Thorvald bursts into Jefferies's apartment. Because of the relationship established between Jefferies and what he watches, the scene carries overtones of a confrontation with a *doppelganger;* or of the eruption of a monstrous force from the underworld of the subconscious, demanding recognition. The effect is made more, not less, frightening by the fact that Thorvald is presented, not as a monster, but as a human being, half terrible, half perplexed and pitiable. If he were merely a monster we could reject him quite comfortably; because our reaction to him is mixed, we have to accept him as representative of potentialities in Jefferies and, by extension, in all of us. In him is adumbrated one of the leading themes of *Psycho,* more clearly here than in any previous Hitchcock film. We watched him, earlier, with Jefferies, through the telephoto objective, washing the axe, wrapping up the saw and carving-knife, then lying down to sleep: our common humanity involves us all in his actions, he is not *only* a brutal murderer, but also a man who has to sleep sometimes, we are left to speculate, to *feel* about, the state of his mind, as we are to be later about the mind of Norman Bates. As he bears down upon Jefferies, a great looming menacing shadow, Jefferies tries to fight him off with his only weapon of defence—his camera, repeatedly loaded with dazzling flash-bulbs—and alternately we are placed subjectively in the positions of Jefferies and the murderer, emphasising his significance as a kind of potential *alter ego.* The flash-bulbs become symbolic: Jefferies's camera is his means of keeping life (which includes his knowledge of himself) at a distance, of remaining a spectator, of preserving his detachment. It takes up the image of Lisa and the lamps. But ultimately it cannot save him: the dazzlement is ineffectual, Thorvald bears down upon him and pushes him headlong over his balcony. Jefferies's victory is, I have said, equivocal: it looks very much like defeat: and with him we hurtle groundwards, terrifyingly, helplessly plunging towards darkness.

But the confrontation is in itself a kind of victory: a clarification—on one level the murderer is exposed and caught, on another Jefferies is ready to accept marriage. He has been confronted by the darkness that Hitchcock sees as underlying—or as surrounding—all human existence: the chaos of our unknown, unrecognized "Under-nature" (a term A.P. Rossiter uses when dis-

74

cussing Shakespeare's tragedies in *Angel with Horns)* which is also the unknownness of the universe. This may strike the reader as an absurdly inflated and pretentious way of talking about a film which is, on the surface, a light comedy-thriller; but I think anyone willing to expose himself to the disturbing undercurrents of the film (as a "light comedy-thriller" it is often found vaguely unsatisfactory because it "leaves a nasty taste") will find it justified. When we emancipate ourselves from a response exclusively on the "comedy-thriller" level, the images—light flashes against the murderer's shadowy bulk—take on great power; moreover, it is impossible not to associate them with Tippi Hedren's struggle to ward off the attacking birds in the attic by waving her torch at them, at the end of *The Birds,* where, whether one likes the film or not, at least a gesture towards metaphysical significance will be allowed. The flash-bulbs (and the torch) sum up for us the inadequacy of human knowledge against this "under-nature". The Hitchcock hero typically lives in a small, enclosed world of his own fabrication, at once a protection and a prison, artificial and unrealistic, into which the "real" chaos erupts, demanding to be faced: consider Henry Fonda's descent into Hell in *The Wrong Man,* or Cary Grant deprived of the security of office and cocktail bar in *North by Northwest.*

The ending of *Rear Window* shows us the achievement of an uneasy equilibrum. Jefferies's development has been made possible through his submitting to a process, the indulging of morbid curiosity and the consequences of that indulgence: a process which in itself is a manifestation of his sickness. Only by following it through does progress become possible for him. At the end, with *both* legs in plaster, he is seated with his back to the window, while Lisa, ostensibly engrossed in a news magazine, surreptitiously reads Harper's Bazaar. None of the problems between them has been solved; but the fact of their engagement, and Jefferies's symbolic back-to-window position, tell us that they have been at least in a sense accepted. Parallel to this, and on one level expressing it, is the resolution of the problems of the various tenants opposite: we see "Miss Torso's" true love coming home, "Miss Lonelyhearts" receiving a nice young man, and so on: to cap it all comes the song-writer's new, saccharine-sweet inspiration, "Lisa". The very neatness of all this tying-up of loose ends emphasizes its superficiality, and we are left with the feeling of the precariousness of it all. The ending is by no means permitted to obliterate for us the memory of the woman's denunciation of the "society" the apartments epitomise, when she finds her dog poisoned: "Was it because he *liked* you?". Nor does the happy ending offset the sense the film, with its stylised presentation of flats and occupants, has established, of semi-live puppets enclosed in little boxes: yet puppets whose frustrations and desperations can drive them to murder or suicide. Order is restored, within and without —in the microcosm of Jefferies's personality, and in the external world which is on one level an extension or reflection of it; but we are left with the feeling that the sweetness-and-light merely covers up that chaos-world that underlies the superficial order.

4. Vertigo

Vertigo seems to me Hitchcock's masterpiece to date, and one of the four or five most profound and beautiful films the cinema has yet given us. This is a claim that may surprise, even amuse, the majority of my readers; but I think an analysis of the film, by revealing an entirely satisfying and fully realised treatment of themes of the most fundamental human significance, can justify it.

The film is adapted from a mystery novel by Boileau and Narcejac—authors also of *Les Diaboliques*—called *D'Entre les Morts:* the two books share the same formula, a squalid exercise in sub-Graham Greenery with a "brilliant" surprise twist at the end that reverses (and in so doing makes nonsense of) the significance of everything that has gone before. Both books are saturated with that easy pessimism that is as much a sentimental self-indulgence as its opposite, characterized by a wilful refusal to see any worthwhile possibilities in human life and human relationships; the characters are either helpless devitalised dupes damned from the outset, or the ingeniously malignant intriguers who trap them. The Clouzot version of *Les Diaboliques* (despite its reversal of the sexes of the original's victim and victimizer) does full justice to the book, the director's temperamental and moral affinity with the authors being continuously in evidence.

Hitchcock took very little from *D'Entre les Morts* apart from the basic plot-line, and then proceeded to minimize the importance even of that. Boileau and Narcejac's cherished surprise solution—the whole *raison d'être* of the book—is revealed to us, in one of the cinema's most daring "alienation effects", about two-thirds of the way through the film; and with lordly indifference to such trivia Hitchcock never bothers to tell us whether or not the murderer gets caught. The objection has frequently been made that the plot hinges on a wild improbability: not so much that a man who has seen the woman he loves fall from a height should not stay to make sure she is dead, as that the murderer should count on his not doing so. But if one is going to approach the film in this way, a moment's thought will make it clear that the whole plot is quite fantastic—no one would ever set about murdering his wife in *that* way. Most of Shakespeare's plays can be demolished in the same way, and with just as much validity. As in Shakespeare's plays, in fact, the organisation of *Vertigo* is thematic; plot, characterisation, psychology, all are strictly subordinated to thematic development.

Whatever aspect we choose to consider, in passing from book to film, we find total transformation. The difference in significance in the locations, for example, is not simply a matter of transposition from France to America: the novel offers no equivalent for the sequoias, and the complex thematic and emotional deepening that comes with them. The characters are quite altered and an important new one (Midge) introduced. Of even greater consequence is the difference in the attitude to them: in Boileau/Narcejac they are despised like so many ignominious worms, and we are invited to look down upon them, and to regard life as squalid and ignoble; in Hitchcock they become entirely acceptable representatives of the human condition, whom we are permitted to regard—for all their weaknesses and limitations—with respect and sympathetic concern: no question here of any failure of awareness of human potentiality, flawed and imperfect as the protagonists may be. The drab, wilful pessimism of *D'Entre les Morts* is an essentially different world from the intense tragic sense of *Vertigo,* which derives from a simultaneous awareness of the immense value of human relationships and their inherent incapability of perfect realisation.

But that *Vertigo* is superior to a poor book does not of course justify my large claims for it, and I must now turn to the film itself. Granted an unfaltering continuity of development, it can be seen to fall conveniently into a brief prologue and three main *acts* or *movements* (I prefer the latter term). The prologue gives us the incident that precipitates Scottie's vertigo; the first movement his consent to watch Madeleine, his following her, the gradual deepening of his involvement; the second takes us from her attempted suicide and their meeting, through their developing relationship to her death and his breakdown; the third begins with his meeting with Judy, and passes through the development of their relationship, his attempted re-creation of Madeleine, to Judy's death and the curing of Scottie's vertigo.

One aspect of the theme of *Vertigo* is given us by Saul Bass's credit designs. We see a woman's face; the camera moves in first to lips, then to eyes. The face is blank, mask-like, representing the inscrutability of appearances: the impossibility of knowing what goes on behind the mask. But the eyes dart nervously from side to side: beneath the mask are imprisoned unknown emotions, fears, desperation. Then a vertiginous, spiralling movement begins in the depths of the eye, moving outwards as if to involve the spectator: before the film proper has begun, we are made aware that the vertigo of the title is to be more than a literal fear of heights. This credit sequence is linked by the music that accompanies it to the scene of Judy's metamorphosis into Madeleine in the beauty salon: the only scene where the same music returns, again as accompaniment to a close-up of a woman's face—a face that is being transformed into a mask.

The first image is of a horizontal bar standing out against a blurred background: a single solid object against an undefined mass. The shot is held for a moment, then two hands grab the bar, the camera moves back, the focus deepens, to reveal a city spread out beneath the night: suggestions of clinging and falling set against a great wilderness of roof-tops. There follows the accident, with Scottie (James Stewart) clinging to a collapsing gutter while a policeman, trying to save him, plunges past him to his death hundreds of feet below. The sensation of vertigo is conveyed to the spectator by the most direct means, subjective shots using a simultaneous zoom-in and track-back that makes the vast drop telescope out before our eyes; we watch, from Scottie's viewpoint, the policeman hurtle down. The sensation has been explained, I believe, by psychologists as arising from the tension between the desire to fall and the dread of falling—an idea it is worth bearing in mind in relation to the whole film. In any case, we, with Scottie, are made to understand what it feels like to be so near death, and to have death made so temptingly easy, yet so terrifying, a way out of pain and effort: to live, he must hold on desperately to the gutter, his arms and body agonisingly stretched, his fingers strained, his mind gripped by unendurable tension; to die, he has only to let go. When we next see Scottie, he is sitting in the apartment of Midge (Barbara Bel Geddes). We do not see, and are never told, how he got down from the gutter: there seems no possible way he *could* have got down. The effect is of leaving him,

79

VERTIGO: top, Scottie (James Stewart) and Midge (Barbara Bel Geddes)—"the ultimate impossibility of getting through to another person in the deepest essentials"; and bottom, Scottie rescues Madeleine (Kim Novak) from drowning.

throughout the film, metaphorically suspended over a great abyss.

Midge and her apartment (that contrasts markedly, we see later, with Scottie's own, which is furnished largely with antiques) represent one of the possibilities before Scottie. The assessment of Midge herself is made with that complexity and economy so characteristic of Hitchcock (though it is only completed by the contrast offered by Madeleine); it is an assessment not only of a clearly defined character but of a whole milieu, even of modern culture itself. It is a very sympathetic portrait: Midge is practical, realistic, emancipated, eminently sane, positive and healthy in her outlook: but from the outset the inadequacies revealed later are hinted at. A trained artist, she devotes her energies to sketching advertisements for brassières. In her cluttered studio-cum-living-room, Miros on the wall are juxtaposed indiscriminately with fashion designs. Entirely devoid of mystery or reserve, the kind of sexuality she represents is suggested by her smart sex-chat about corsets and brassières ("You know about those things, you're a big boy now"), she reduces everything to the same matter-of-fact level. Yet one senses already a discrepancy between what she is and what she might be: a depth of feeling, of constancy, is hinted at, more visually than verbally, which is at odds with the superficiality of the cultural environment her flat evokes. Her look at Scottie when he reminds her that it was she who broke off their three-week-long engagement is one of those moments that reveal the basic strength of the cinema, because it suggests things not really formulable in words: one could say that the rest of the film defines why she broke it off. If there is something a little boyish about her, there is also something—Scottie actually uses the word—"motherly". She reminds one a little of that other sympathetic young-mother figure, the Doris Day of *The Man Who Knew Too Much*: she disapproves of Scottie's leaving the police, she supervises his attempt to "lick" his vertigo (by climbing her portable steps) as a mother

81

might help a child to master a bicycle, alternately urging and restraining.

He tells her, in his habitually non-committal manner, that he is still available—"That's me, available Ferguson"; the phrase recalls his decision to "do nothing" to give us the full extent of his "availability" and suggests one aspect of that metaphorical suspension: he is suspended both in work and in personal relationships. That characteristic Hitchcockian economy and directness in organisation connects this "availability" with Elster, whom Scottie goes on at once to mention. The scene ends with the attempt to overcome the vertigo, culminating in the startling subjective shot of the street over which Scottie hung, which he sees again when he looks down from the top of Midge's steps. In the foreground of the shot, we see ornaments and a bowl of flowers that keep the reality of Midge's room before us; but that reality—Midge's world, charming, uncomplicated, safe, superficial—is shattered by the vision. Scottie has seen death, and the experience has undermined all possibility of his accepting Midge and the life she represents as adequate fulfilment. It is Midge's room that becomes unreal, the vision (a great abyss apparently in the middle of that room) that is "real". Hitchcock cuts from her "motherly" frightened comforting of him to the exterior of Elster's offices.

What I have called the *thematic* organisation of the film can be seen in the transition from the smart modernity of Midge's apartment to the discussion about the past in Elster's office. Behind Elster we see shipbuilding in progress, and there is a model ship in the room, carrying a suggestion of escape. The walls are covered with prints of San Francisco in the "old days": Scottie and Elster examine one as they talk. Elster bears a clear thematic relationship to Scottie. Shipbuilding—modern development —bores him; he has a nostalgia for the past, where a man had "freedom" and "power": the words are echoed twice later in the film, in the bookshop (linking Elster with the man who destroyed Carlotta Valdes) and at the end. There is in Elster a hint of the inexplicable—of the diabolical—in his intuitive understanding of Scottie's psychological traits (the metaphorical, as well as the literal, vertigo), in his fastening on them and *using* them: at the end of the film, Scottie's insistent question, "Why did you pick on me? Why *me?*" never gets an explicit answer. Elster, like other Hitchcock villains (Bruno Anthony, for example), besides being a clearly defined character in his own right, is related to a weakness in the hero. We shall see how important for Scottie are a nostalgia for the past and a desire for "freedom" and "power".

The long expository dialogue between the two men is given tension by the sense conveyed of Elster's control of Scottie's responses, and by the exactness in the use of cutting and camera-movement to express that control. In a cut to close-up we see the effect on Scottie of Elster's abrupt, unobtrusive "Someone dead" (in answer to Scottie's question as to who may harm Elster's wife); then the camera immediately moves back to take in Elster standing over him, dominating, *imposing* his story. Scottie rejects it: he is "the hard-headed Scot": but rejects it, with his insistent reiteration that all the wife needs is a psychologist, too emphatically. We are very much aware of the tension in him between natural scepticism and an attraction towards the fantastic story, with its associations of Elster's wife with the past and with death. Madeleine, Elster tells him, sits by a lake looking at pillars across the water, pillars that are called "The Portals of the Past". The "wandering" theme—picked up both verbally and visually many times later in the film—the theme of being lost in life, of having no clear aim—is stated here by Elster ("She wanders—God knows where she wanders"). It is natural to link it with Scottie's expressed lack of purpose (his "doing nothing") and hence with the "vertigo" idea. He is sufficiently intrigued to agree at least to see Madeleine before he rejects the case.

There follows about quarter of an hour without dialogue, showing us the growth of Scottie's obsession with Madeleine. She herself is introduced by a camera-movement different from any that has preceded it, that sets a new mood, maintained throughout the ensuing sequences up to Scottie's next meeting with Midge. We are in Ernie's, the restaurant where Scottie is to see Madeleine. Close-up of Scottie seated at the bar, looking across. The camera swings over in a slow, graceful movement disclosing the *décor* of the restaurant, which evokes immediately the gracious living of the past, then tracks slowly in towards a table, gradually focussing our attention on the bare back of a woman in evening dress leaning in a graceful attitude, almost statuesque. Then, in a subjective shot from Scottie's viewpoint, we watch her cross the restaurant with an easy, gliding motion, and pause near him so that her face is clearly visible, beautiful, smooth, without definable expression.

The fascination Madeleine exerts over Scottie—and over us—is complex. One is immediately aware of the contrast between her and Midge. Where Midge is an entirely known quantity, Madeleine is surrounded by an aura of mystery. She is always remote from Scottie and from us: we see her only as Scottie sees her. When she goes to a flower-shop, she enters by a back door, down a side street, passing through dingy, cobwebby store-rooms; later, she apparently disappears from a house: she may be herself a ghost. She represents a completely different sexuality from Midge's: one has only to compare Midge's demonstrating the latest brassière "based on the principle of the Cantilever Bridge", with Madeleine's hesitant grace of movement and attitude later as she comes to stand in the doorway of Scottie's sitting-room wearing his dressing-gown: Madeleine is so much more erotic because of this combination of grace, mysteriousness and vulnerability. She is from the start the representative of another world, of experience beyond the grasp of the cards-on-the-table reality of Midge. A higher reality, or an illusion? Or, to shift to the Keatsian terminology, "vision", or "waking dream"? It seems more reasonable to adduce *Lamia* or the Nightingale Ode in this connection than to make the conventional classification of *Vertigo* as "mystery-thriller";

84

and it is worth pointing out that we find in Hitchcock a far more secure and mature balance of sympathy and interest between the real world and the visionary, and certainly a no less complex awareness of the issues, than Keats was capable of. If it be objected that Madeleine does in fact turn out to be pure illusion, I shall answer that the matter is by no means so simple.

Madeleine certainly is presented as a dream, in some sense; and she becomes our dream as well as Scottie's. If her own movements, in their grace, their air of remoteness, are dream-like, the effect of dream is intensified by Hitchcock's use of the camera. Leisurely, steady-paced subjective tracking-shots characterize the sequences in which Scottie follows Madeleine; we are placed behind the windscreen of his car in the driver's seat as he follows her around the streets of San Francisco, pursuing a dream through modern surface-reality; we wander at his walking-pace round the graveyard; we watch Madeleine continually through his eyes, her distance, her silence, his and our inability to understand her, help her, protect her, are all a part of the fascination. The effect of romantic dream is especially strong in the churchyard sequence, everything steeped in hazy sunlight as Madeleine stands, statue-like, minute in long-shot, over an unknown grave.

The settings to which she leads Scottie (Spanish church, graveyard, art gallery, old house) in and around San Francisco, seem nonetheless not to belong to the city, they are little pockets of silence and solitude, another world. She leads him back always to the past—the grave, the portrait, the house of a long-dead woman. Finally, and perhaps most important of all, she is continually associated with death, and the fascination she exerts is the fascination of death, a drawing towards oblivion and final release; the yearning for the dream, for the Ideal, for the Infinite, become logically a yearning for death: Scottie's and our vertigo.

This death-wish—or more exactly, in "vertigo" terms, the simultaneous longing for and fear of death—culminates in the scene among the sequoia trees: "the oldest living thing". The dialogue stresses the fear:

SCOTTIE: "What are you thinking about?"

MADELEINE: "All the people who were born and died while the trees went on living . . ."

SCOTTIE: "Its real name is Sequoia Sempreviva".

MADELEINE: "I don't like it . . . Knowing I have to die".

They examine a cross-section of a felled tree. The camera moves across it, outwards from the core, taking us through centuries in seconds; Madeleine puts her fingers tentatively near the circumference, murmuring, "Somewhere here I was born, and there I died. It was only a moment for you, you took no notice". She moves off, and disappears among the trees. Disappears, as she previously disappeared in the Carlotta Valdes house: Scottie follows but can't find her, and we get a slow, sinuous tracking-shot of "ever-living" tree-trunks and sunlight which precisely realises the significance of the quoted dialogue, the pitiful brevity and transience of the individual life most beautifully and disturbingly conveyed. The whole scene is bathed in an atmosphere of romantic dream—its great visual beauty intensified by the emotional overtones, by the whole con-text—which counterpoints the dread of death expressed in the dialogue with a sense of yearning for peace and oblivion.

The sequence culminates in the kiss by the sea, the mutual capitulation to love. From Scottie's point of view, the significance of this *as* a culmination is clear—his love for Madeleine becomes identified with his death-yearning. Earlier, gazing in his car at a reproduction of the Carlotta Valdes portrait, he saw the dead woman and Madeleine as interchangeable (in terms of film, dissolve from the portrait to Madeleine and back). On one level there is a strong element of romantic cliché in the image of the lovers embracing against a background of crashing waves, an effect which crystallises for us another aspect of the film: for many spectators, the cinema itself is a kind of dream, an escape-world in which reality can be evaded and forgotten. In one way Hitchcock is throughout the first half of *Vertigo* using his audience's escapist expectations, the fact that they go to the cinema in order to see a "hero" with whom they can identify, involved in romantic wish-fulfilments: hence at this climactic moment dream and romantic cliché merge. But, at a deeper level, the sea as the culmination of this part of the film has another significance: if the sequoia trees are "the oldest living thing", the sea is older still, beating eternally against the rocks, eroding, wearing down; and it is against such sea-associations that the two embrace on the cliff-edge, a tiny, precarious moment placed against eternity. But this is perhaps merely to suggest why the cliché itself still has emotional validity.

Before this sequence there has occurred the nearest to a meeting between Midge and Madeleine that ever takes place: Midge, driving up to Scottie's apartment, sees Madeleine drive away. That the two women never appear, beyond this, in the same scene brings home to us the incompatibility of the worlds they represent. Midge's reappearance immediately after the beautiful sensitive, tentative groping towards a relationship between Scottie and Madeleine, makes us aware of her exclusion from certain levels of experience and her inadequacy to combat the sort of rivalry Madeleine offers; yet at the same time it makes us aware of her as representing a healthy normality to set against the element of neurotic sickness in Scottie's attraction to Madeleine. Now, after the sequoia sequence, we have the scene in Midge's apartment where she shows Scottie the parody-portrait of herself as Carlotta. She is trying to make him see *her,* to substitute herself for the woman who obsesses him, at the same time making the obsession ridiculous by satirizing it, and the attempt reveals both her anti-romantic down-to-earth normality and her inadequacy. It finally destroys Scottie's connection with her: he resents the attempt to shatter the dream. There is a marvellous shot, superbly balanced between pathos and humour, of Midge seated beside her self-portrait, the two images in the same attitude, the Carlotta portrait with Midge's unglamorous, bespectacled face; but the figure in the portrait holds the posy Madeleine carried with her through the graveyard and the art gallery, and Midge's hands are empty. The portrait is Midge's attempt at an "alienation effect", its purpose the breaking of an involvement; but its effect is to alienate Scottie from *her*. We recall the moment in his car when the image of Madeleine was superimposed on the portrait reproduction. Reality is defeated, the dream is too strong; and Midge is left tearing her hair, alone with her sense of inadequacy.

There follows the sequence at the Mission of San Juan Baptista, culminating in Madeleine's suicide. Here, in the livery-stable, amid the *décor* of the past, Scottie makes his last effort to explain the dream, to make it reality. The suicide itself has a shattering effect on the spectator which is by no means to be explained solely in terms of visual impact, strong as this is—the bell-tower, the unnerving "vertigo" shots down the stair-well, the body falling past the aperture then spread out lifeless on the roof below. On one level, again, we have Hitchcock capitalising on audience expectations by abruptly defeating them: no one, I think, seeing *Vertigo* for the first time unprepared, thinks that Madeleine is going to die halfway through. She is the heroine of the romance, the medium through which the escape-wishes are to be fulfilled: we are prepared for a happy ending, or perhaps for final grand tragedy, but not for this brutal mid-way rupture. But Madeleine, as I have suggested, represents wish-fulfilment on a deeper and more valid level than that normally offered by the Hollywood film: by this point in the film she has evoked in us all that longing for something beyond daily reality which is so basic to human nature. We are in fact by this time so thoroughly identified with Scottie that we share his shock, and the resulting sense of bewildered desolation, in the most direct way, just as we share his sense of helplessness, even of responsibility. We are stunned, the bottom is knocked out of the world, we cannot at all see where the film is going, what possible sequel this event can have: all is chaos. It is an effect that Hitchcock is to match, two films later, in *Psycho* with the shower-bath murder.

We have already been placed, then, in a position to understand, sympathetically, Scottie's breakdown. It is preceded by the inquest, in which a brutal coronor places the responsibility for Madeleine's death on him, and which closes with the shot of his leaving the courtroom, a vast expanse of ceiling seeming to weigh down oppressively over the tiny figures in long-shot.

The breakdown is precipitated by Scottie's nightmare. This begins with an image of disintegration from earlier in the film—the posy which Madeleine plucked to pieces, dropped in the water and watched floating away immediately before her first suicide attempt. Again the posy (suggestive of a tight, unnatural order) disintegrates, only in the dream Hitchcock uses cartoon—crude cartoon at that—to show it: the image of real flowers turned to paper flowers suggests that the possibility that the whole Madeleine ideal is a fraud is already nightmarishly present in Scottie's subconscious. The next dream image goes back to the inquest, with Scottie and Gavin Elster by the courtroom window, but now Carlotta Valdes stands between them, dressed as in the portrait. Carlotta now "possesses" Madeleine as completely as Mrs. Bates possesses Norman at the end of *Psycho:* possesses her in death. Madeleine's identitification with the portrait (one of the sources of her fascination) is now complete, and the essential paradox of Scottie's desires crystallised: he has sought an identification of reality and dream, of life and death, and now there is only the face from the portrait looking at him tauntingly. The image also intensifies the sense of the possibility of fraud, because of its incongruity: Gavin Elster and the supernatural simply don't belong in the same world (or in the same shot), and the image tells us—retrospectively at least—that we should never have trusted his story. With the elliptical logic of dream, we next have Scottie walking, purposefully yet in a void, without seeming to know where he is going yet unable to stop; walking through the graveyard; walking to Carlotta's now open grave. We become him by means of camera-identification, and fall forward into the grave, into darkness, a bottomless pit. The subsequent images prolong the falling sensation, until we see the *man's* body falling on to the roof where Madeleine fell; but the roof dissolves and he hurtles into endless space, blindingly white. Scottie wakes up screaming. Here, at the centre of the film, is the clearest statement about the nature of the "vertigo". In his dream he achieves identity with Madeleine: first by sinking into her grave (as described by her earlier in the scene by the sea), then by falling on to the roof. He wants to die in her place, or to join her in death; but looking back we can see his whole attraction to her as a matter of identification—the desire for annihilation. The continued use of subjective technique during the nightmare serves both to render Scottie's sensations (hence his breakdown) directly comprehensible, and to make us experience the logical outcome of our identification with his basic driving impulse. We may think back to Scottie's, and our, vision of the street during the attempted cure in Midge's room: the film conveys a terrifying impression of external reality as a sort of fragile shell which we pierce at our peril: once beyond it, we are whirling uncontrolled in chaos. We may be led to think back, in turn, to the credit designs: the mask-like face of Appearance, the vertiginous, spiralling movement drawing us down into the depths behind the eye.

The scene in the mental home in which Midge tries to break through to a Scottie completely withdrawn into melancholia makes us view him objectively, look in the face the condition into which his alienation from reality has led him. Music-lovers will wince at the use of Mozart here—his music clearly identified with the superficial externality of Midge's world—but objections on musical grounds are hardly relevant. The point of the music, its total inability to reach Scottie, lost as he is in the abyss he has fallen into, is defined by its context, and in fact the very superficial and shallow interpretation of the andante of the 34th symphony (taken at a ridiculously brisk tempo) that Midge plays him fulfils its function admirably. The music as played suggests both a poise and an artificiality that admirably epitomises for us the fragile shell.

The scene ends with Midge's acknowledgement of defeat. After moving around the entirely passive and immobile Scottie, vainly caressing him ("You're not lost— Mother's here"), she takes off the gramophone record and tells the doctor, "I don't think Mozart's going to help at all": a line given great poignance by the actress's delivery, which conveys her sense not only of Mozart's inadequacy but of her own. We see her—it is her last appearance in the film—walk away down the hospital corridor; and as she reaches the end the screen darkens around her, so that the darkness seems to swallow her. This is a unifying image of great importance. It recalls immediately the shot of Scottie descending the bell-tower stairs after Madeleine's death, where the camera, pointing straight down into the well, made it look like a tunnel into which the figure, moving away from the camera, was disappearing. By linking the two moments visually Hitchcock draws our attention to a similarity beyond the visual, as a means of universalising his themes. At both points in question the person disappearing has failed to help or save the person he or she loves: both have been made aware of the ultimate impossibility of getting through to another person in the deepest essentials. And in both cases a relationship has been irreparably broken on whose continuance and development future happiness and fulfilment seemed entirely dependent. But there is another, perhaps more obvious link: the dream which Madeleine described to Scottie as they stood by the sea: ". . . walking down a long corridor . . . When I come to the end there's nothing but darkness". There is also a grave—"an open grave. It's my grave"—the grave which swallowed Scottie into darkness in the nightmare. With the two visual links, the corridor image takes on a universal symbolism, connecting all three principal characters, exposing that point at which

91

VERTIGO: the bell-tower

every human being is essentially alone, beyond the help of others. If I point to the clear link (through bell-tower and nightmare) with the "vertigo" theme, the full force of the word "organic" applied to *Vertigo* will perhaps be felt. To anticipate, it is the significance that has accrued to the corridor image that gives the scene of Madeleine's re-creation—Judy's return from the beauty salon with face and hair transformed—such emotional intensity: she appears at the end of the hotel corridor in the light, walking towards Scottie (us), precisely reversing the previous corridor images and thereby intensifying that effect of resurrection that is the more poignant in that we know it, then, (as Scottie doesn't) to be in normal senses illusory.

That phrase "normal senses" will seem either willfully mysterious or merely vague; but the qualification it implies will soon become clear. We enter now the third movement of the film, and the revelation that drastically alters—at first glance simplifies, at second renders enormously more complex—most of what has gone before. Scottie, partially recovered but still obsessed by Madeleine, wanders around the places she frequented, seeing her in other women—imposing the dream on reality. Then he sees a girl in the street who bears little superficial resemblance to Madeleine (unlike the other women)—indeed, seems to provide on the surface, in clothes, make-up, manner, gestures, way of moving, nothing but contrast—yet whose face is sufficiently like Madeleine's for Scottie to follow her to her hotel room. Her first appearance is introduced by a shot of a flower-shop window with, prominently displayed, posies identical to the one Madeleine carried, the posy that changed into disintegrating paper flowers in Scottie's nightmare. Five minutes later we see, in flashback showing the girl Judy's memory, what really happened: she was Madeleine, Madeleine was a fraud, the body falling past the aperture a woman Scottie has never seen. Two big questions are now raised: why did Hitchcock choose to break the first law of the mystery-thriller and divulge the "surprise" solution two-thirds of the way through the film? And what differences does the revelation make, in retrospect, to the significance of what has preceded it? I shall leave the answer to the first question—which primarily affects the last third of the film—aside for the moment and try to answer the second.

Our immediate reaction to the revelation, I think, is extreme disappointment. This can exist on a purely superficial level: we have come to see a mystery story and now we know it all, so what is the use of the film's continuing? Why should we have to watch the detective laboriously discovering things we know already? Much popular discontent with the film can be traced to this premature revelation, and in terms of audience-reaction it was certainly a daring move on Hitchcock's part. Yet our feelings of being cheated, if we analyse them, reveal a deeper cause. We have been, up to the revelation, very largely identified with Scottie, we have involved ourselves deeply in his weaknesses and his desires, in his longing to fulfil a dream as a means of escaping from or of rising above daily reality. We experienced directly his shock at Madeleine's death: now we experience a further, and worse shock: not only is she dead—she never existed. The effect is not merely of discovering that we have been deceived by an ingenious murder plot: one of our most vulnerable moral spots, our discontent with reality, has been penetrated, we have been caught off our guard. Some of the best films that have come from Hollywood, films as different in tone and in overt subject-matter as Howard Hawks's *Monkey Business* and Nicholas Ray's *Bigger Than Life,* have had as their core this theme of discontent with the actual world, but none has explored it as profoundly or brought it home to the spectator by such direct, inescapable means, as *Vertigo.* The revelation cuts the ground away from under our feet, and makes us painfully aware of the degree of our previous involvement in what is now proved to be a cheap hoax.

Yet this reaction, which the film certainly provokes at this point, has to be modified on reflection. If we re-see the film, or carefully reconstruct the first two-thirds, we shall see that we have not yet taken the full measure of

VERTIGO:
Scottie with
Madeleine
(above) and
Judy (below).

the subtlety and complexity of Hitchcock's conception. For such a re-viewing or reconstruction will show us that the illusion is not *just* an illusion: Judy was not *merely* acting Madeleine—up to a point she *became* Madeleine. Our very incredulity that the Judy we see could ever have been trained to act the part of Madeleine works for Hitchcock here. Judy—on her first appearance, and in her treatment of Scottie when he follows her to her hotel room—appears hard and vulgar, over made-up, her attitude at once defiant and cheaply provocative; she is playing up the tartiness to deceive him, and her underlying vulnerability is gradually exposed, yet she is never depicted as intelligent. But she was, as Scottie tells her at the end of the film, "a very apt pupil". If we mentally juxtapose her stance and manner in the doorway of the hotel room—her way of holding her body, her expression, her intonation, her vulgarised version of what is in part their love story—with, again, Madeleine's entry from Scottie's bedroom, her way of moving and standing, her hesitant words, her reticence and *pudeur,* we shall see that Madeleine was not just an acted role but another *persona*.

It is not difficult to see that the pretence partly became reality. Most obviously, there is the point that Judy was to make Scottie fall in love with her by pretending to fall in love with him, and then she really *did* fall in love. Her behaviour before the "suicide" is full of obvious ambiguities ("It wasn't supposed to happen this way . . . If you love me, you'll know I loved you and I wanted to go on loving you"—the remarks mean something quite different depending on whether we think of them as spoken by Madeleine or by Judy), and if we look further we shall see that in fact every moment of the relationship is ambiguous, it is impossible to distinguish pretence from reality. Is her nervousness during the car journey to San Juan Baptista real or feigned—Judy pretending to be Madeleine becoming distraught, or Judy becoming distraught as she gets nearer to what she has agreed to do? Her scream as Mrs. Elster falls, the scream Scottie so insistently questions her about at the end: is it the scream that was (presumably) planned to accompany the fall, or the scream of a woman trying, too late, to prevent an outrage at which she has connived?

Madeleine says to Scottie, "One shouldn't live alone . . . It's wrong": Judy lives alone. Later, by the sea, telling Scottie her fragments of memory: ". . . A room. I sit there alone—always alone". The room in the McKittrick hotel, of course. Or Judy's hotel room? We see Madeleine once when Scottie can't see her—as she watches him from her car going to close the door of his apartment before they drive out to the sequoias: she is watching him tenderly, sadly, as if attracted to him—is she still acting? When he tries to make her tell him, under the trees, why she jumped into the Bay, she appears to panic, reiterating "Please don't ask me, please don't ask me": again, Judy pretending to be a woman on the verge of breakdown, or Judy falling in love and terrified at the situation she is in? And the fears of death: when Madeleine says, "I don't want to die—there's someone within me says I must die", she could be speaking for Judy, for all of us; she is not only Judy pretending to be Madeleine possessed by Carlotta. Yet Judy, we feel (the Judy of the last third of the film), is not a girl who would ever allow herself to become explicit about, perhaps even conscious of, such fears: she hasn't the intelligence, the self-awareness, or (despite her evident capacity for suffering) the depth. The fears can only be released in her through her being Madeleine: in a sense, it is Madeleine who is the more "real" of the two, since in Madeleine all kinds of potentialities completely hidden in Judy find expression. The pretence was that Carlotta was taking possession of Madeleine; in reality, Madeleine has taken possession of Judy. Scottie and Madeleine are linked verbally—at many points—by the fact that both are "wanderers" (with all the overtones the word accrues in the course of the film). In fact, it becomes clear that Judy as well, in surrendering to the Madeleine identity, is abandoning herself to the fulfilment of a dream. There is, up to the revelation, only one subjective shot from Judy/Madeleine's viewpoint, and

97

it clinches this thematic connection between her and
Scottie: the shot, as she stands by the water before flinging
herself in, of the torn flowers drifting away on the current
—the disintegration-symbol of Scottie's dream. The shot
can also be taken as an imaginative-subjective shot from
Scottie's viewpoint: he can't *see* the flowers drifting away
from where he is standing, but he can see Madeleine tearing and throwing them. So the shot links the two conscious-
nesses, and we are made to feel that the image has much
the same significance for both. With this, and Judy's
absorption in Madeleine, in mind, it is an easy step to
see an *element* of reality in all her supposedly artificial
behaviour. We cannot say that Madeleine's attempted
suicide, her fears of madness, express nothing of Judy
The painfully limited, enclosed Judy, in fact, becomes
articulate in Madeleine, whose *potential* reality to some
extent validates the dream she represents. The theme of
unstable identity is reflected in Scottie, the "wanderer"
who is going to "do nothing": he is "Johnny" or "Johnny
O" to Midge, "John" to Madeleine, "Scottie" to Judy: the
identity is created in part by the relationship.

The "vertigo" of the title, then, expands from one man's
fear of heights into a metaphysical principle, and the
metaphysic of the film is "peculiarly terrifying". I am
thinking of T. E. Eliot's remarks about Blake, where he
speaks of Blake's "peculiarity" as revealing itself as "the
peculiarity of all great poetry . . . It is merely a peculiar
honesty which, in a world too frightened to be honest, is
peculiarly terrifying." (He also remarks that this honesty "is
never present without great technical accomplishment")
The world—human life, relationships, individual identity—
becomes a quicksand, unstable, constantly shifting, into
which we may sink at any step in any direction, illusion
and reality constantly ambiguous, even interchangeable
To such a response to life, Hitchcock's authoritarian attitude to film-making, each film predestined down to the
smallest detail before shooting starts, each camera-move
ment and camera-angle rigorously thought out, the actor
98

strictly controlled, nothing left to chance, is clearly relevant.

Why did Hitchcock divulge the solution so early? Clearly, the decision entailed sacrifices, and not only on the "popular thriller" level: if the spectator's identification with Scottie had been preserved to the end, so that we identified throughout his attempt to re-create Madeleine from Judy, the fascination of the "dream" would also have been preserved, and only at the very end would we have been left stranded with "reality", to leave the cinema in some perplexity. Imagine the last half-hour of the film with the "revelation" scene cut out: we would be in a position to share Scottie's feelings towards Judy very exactly, our interest in her restricted to the lurking suggestion there of Madeleine. We would have shared (as she undergoes her transformation) Scottie's wonder at her resemblance to Madeleine, and like him we would have been torn between surrender to the re-created dream and suspicion of the possibility of some cruel fraud. The Hitchcockian "suspense", in short, with its characteristic undercurrent of moral division, would have held us to the end. Yet the very act of imagining the film without the revelation will convince the spectator of the rightness of Hitchcock's decision.

First, more obviously, the effect of the revelation is to detach us from Scottie's consciousness: suddenly, and for the first time in the film, we know something about Madeleine that he doesn't know. From here on we shall be watching him as much as watching *with* him. But our involvement with him has been such that this is in essence like watching ourselves, and what we see is again, right up to the final clarification, deeply ambiguous: simultaneous drives towards sickness and towards health. As Scottie re-creates Madeleine, is he impelled by a desire to rebuild a dream in which he can lose himself, or by an undeviating (though obscure) determination to reach the truth? If the former is the more obvious, the latter is, as we shall see, indisputably expressed in the film, which offers a particularly beautiful example of that Hitchcockian

99

sense of the inextricability, in human life, of good and evil. Like Jefferies in *Rear Window* Scottie can achieve health (or, if you prefer, enlightenment) only by following through to the end an obsession that has its source in a spiritual sickness. We could have been made (as we were in *Rear Window)* to share in this process; Hitchcock elected to have us study it.

Why this is in this case the better alternative arises from the second difference the revelation makes. Without it, Judy would remain, necessarily, as inscrutable as Madeleine had been; with it, we are constantly made aware of her feelings as well as of Scottie's. The gain in richness and complexity is great; the sacrifice in "suspense" is compensated for by a gain in poignancy that makes this last part of the film profoundly disturbing to watch, by a tension set up in the mind of the spectator between conflicting responses. Knowing the truth, we also have far more opportunity, during the last part of the film, to consider the implications of what we see.

The detachment itself is achieved with a startling abruptness: some find the introduction of the flashback very clumsy, but it seems to me that the abrupt brutality is essential to the effect. Throughout the middle part of the film—since Madeleine's "death"—we have been feeling increasingly at sea. We can't see where the film is going—where Scottie is going. There seems no firm ground, no sense of direction: in fact, we are being made to share Scottie's state of mind once again. Then, suddenly, we are in the room alone with Judy: the withdrawal of Scottie from the scene is like the withdrawal of our own consciousness, we have nothing to cling to. Then the screen darkens around Judy and the flashback begins. Few moments in the cinema produce a greater *frisson:* this rather cheap shallow-seeming girl is suddenly associated with Madeleine's dash up into the church tower. We experience a moment of total bewilderment in which all sense of reality seems terrifyingly to dissolve; then, abruptly, the vertigo is over for us: over, anyway, until we begin to reflect on the quicksand of reality and illusion the film presents.

We watch Judy compose her letter to Scottie, and the intolerability of her situation comes homes to us. She is deeply in love with him, while he is still in love with Madeleine; yet she *is* Madeleine—or Madeleine is potentially within her. As she writes her letter the camera half circles her, and the shade on her table-lamp fills a large area of the screen, at one point obliterating her. The image recalls the scene where Madeleine came to Scottie at dawn to tell him her dream. She sat at his writing-table, leaning forward in the light from his table-lamp as she described her terror of "darkness". The effect was of the pitiful inadequacy of human illumination to combat the enveloping metaphysical darkness (compare the flash-bulbs in *Rear Window* and the torch in *The Birds)*. By linking the two scenes through this image (the lamp and shade get great visual emphasis in both) Hitchcock links Judy's present situation and her inability to cope with it with Madeleine's "darkness". Later, Judy (now dressed like Madeleine but still a brunette) sits in Scottie's room where Madeleine sat in the earlier scene, the light on her as it was on Madeleine. The two scenes also resemble each other in that in both Scottie stands over her in a dominating attitude: in the earlier sequence he was trying to compel the dream to become real, in the later he is trying to compel the reality to become a dream.

After Judy has torn up the letter she hides Madeleine's grey suit right at the back of her cupboard, selecting a dress as unlike it as possible: is she afraid Scottie might see it? Or is she vehemently rejecting her Madeleine identity? Later, in the dress-shop, when Scottie buys her the clothes she wore as Madeleine, her attitude ("No, I won't *do* it . . . I don't *like* it") betrays panic: is she afraid Scottie will learn the truth if she dresses like Madeleine? Or does the thought of slipping back into being Madeleine, the sense of dissolving identity, terrify her?

Throughout these scenes, our consciousness is split between the two characters. By means of this split, Hitchcock makes us aware of the painfulness of the relationship, the tension of which becomes a distillation of the tensions in all human relationships. Scottie can neither accept nor even really *see* the "real" Judy: all that holds him to her is the ghost of Madeleine that lurks within her. He takes her to Ernie's, where he first saw Madeleine. While he gazes fascinated at a woman who, until she gets near, in her movements, figure and clothes resembles Madeleine, the woman who was (and, somewhere, still is?) the real Madeleine sits helplessly, ignored—he "doesn't even know she is there", as Midge said of him in the mental hospital. Judy, in fact, has now taken over from Midge in some respects: it is she, now, who fights, as unsuccessfully as Midge, to keep him in the "real" world. Her insistence that he see *her,* that he like *her,* reminds us of Midge's clumsy attempt to destroy the dream with the portrait. The irony of the scene in Ernie's brings home to us forcefully that Scottie has not been in love with a woman so much as with—almost in the Platonic sense— an Idea. Later Scottie takes Judy walking by a lake: it was the first thing associated with Madeleine, the lake Garvin Elster described her as sitting by, gazing across at the pillars we now see—the appropriately named "Portals of the Past". Judy yearningly watches couples kissing on the bank: Scottie isn't even holding her hand. Later, in his apartment, she tells him, "You don't even want to touch me". By now, the film has defined very thoroughly all that was behind that look of Midge's when Scottie reminded her that it was she who broke off their engagement. But, if Scottie represents an extreme case (we classify him by now, certainly, as a sick man), this rejection of life for an unattainable Idea is something fundamental in human nature, his sickness still, potentially, our sickness. The tendency in relationships to form an idealised image of the other person and substitute it for the reality is relevant here.

But it is during the sequences showing Scottie's attempt to turn Judy into Madeleine that the emotional effect of our feeling *with* both of them at once rises to its greatest intensity. In Scottie we see revealed the duality of impulse I mentioned earlier. When Judy asks him "What good will it do?" his "I don't know" is clearly genuine: he is not *only* bent on re-creating a dream. In Judy we watch the gradual submergence of her identity as her Madeleine *persona* is re-assumed. As she sinks down on to the cushions Scottie places for her before his fire—the cushions he placed there earlier for Madeleine—we sense her awareness that she is slipping helplessly into something she won't be able to control. As he waits for her to emerge from her bedroom with her hair up—the final item in the re-creation—we see in his face a fear mixed with longing, a nagging doubt and uneasiness. The bedroom door opens, and the camera remains on her face. For a moment he can't bring himself to look round at her: if what he sees *is* Madeleine, then Madeleine was a hoax. When she appears, we see her through his eyes, dazzling but blurred, a realised dream. As Judy, now Madeleine again, moves forward to him, her face expressing a beautifully erotic yearning, we see that it is not only clothes and hairstyle that have changed: her way of moving is different, her expression again has Madeleine's sensitivity. There follows the kiss during which the camera performs a 360° tracking movement around them. In the middle of it, Hitchcock back-projects behind them the carriage in the livery-stable at San Juan Baptista. Past and present, illusion and reality, merge. It is at once the triumph of illusion, the perfect re-creation of the dream, and the expression of the painful nagging doubt that necessarily accompanies the sense that this is indeed Madeleine. During the kiss we see Scottie's face troubled and perplexed, divided between surrender and suspicion; while Madeleine clings to him as she clung to him when they kissed by the sea, seeming to hang on him for help, protection, security, as if drowning.

When Judy/Madeleine re-enters after dressing for dinner, it is Madeleine we see moving. Madeleine we hear talking: Judy is quite submerged. She wants to go to Ernie's ("Well, after all, it's our place"). She has re-entered the Madeleine world. When she makes the fatal, apparently so stupid and obvious, mistake of putting on

103

the Carlotta Valdes necklace and asking Scottie to link it for her, it is simply the final surrender of her identity as Judy: *she* is Madeleine again. We are shown Scottie's realisation subjectively: the necklace on Judy's throat in the mirror is juxtaposed with the same necklace in Carlotta's portrait. Because we have long since known the truth, we cannot share his shock of comprehension, though the use of identification-technique helps us to understand it.

But there is more to this beautiful moment than that. From the close-up of the necklace around Carlotta's neck the camera tracks back to take in Madeleine staring in the art gallery, her posy beside her: the shot draws together with poignant effect various strands of emotional reaction: our (and Scottie's) past feeling for the dream locks with our present feeling for (and Scottie's bitter reaction against) Judy. Also, the backward tracking-shot contrasts with the frequent forward tracking-shots that characterized the earlier part of the film, to suggest recoil, Scottie extricating himself from the quicksands of illusion. The earlier shots in the art gallery took him (and us) forward into the dream, tracking in on the posies, and on the similarly styled hair, of Madeleine and Carlotta, hair arranged in a spiral that evoked the patterns of the credit-titles and the whole vertigo theme. Now the camera sweeps back: the effect is in some ways analogous to that of the car re-emerging from the swamp at the end of *Psycho*.

The ending of the film perfectly knots all the strands. Scottie's vertigo is cured, not by forcing himself to go higher, nor by the "emotional shock" that Midge told him might do it (he had that the first time Madeleine died), but by finally learning the whole truth: after he has forced the confession from Judy, he can look down the well of the tower without dizziness: the symbolic nature of the vertigo is thus finally emphasised. Judy's death, on the face of it an accident, contains elements both of murder and suicide. It is clear, as he drags her up the tower stairs, that he wants to kill her—he takes her by the throat and shakes her violently. He hates her for

104

not being Madeleine—for destroying for him the possibility of escape into fantasy. Even after he knows the whole truth, he can still cry out bitterly, "I loved you so, Madeleine", without being aware of the name he is using. As for Judy, she protests frantically and yet allows herself to be dragged up the stairs. During and after her confession, we have a terrifying sense of watching a personality disintegrate before our eyes: she talks sometimes as Madeleine, sometimes as Judy. We remember Madeleine's cry to Scottie after the sequoia sequence: "If I'm mad, that would explain it". She is already quite broken before she falls. As for the nun, there is really no need to read any Catholic significance into her. We see her through Judy's eyes rise up like a ghost, and Judy falls, destroyed by Madeleine's return from the dead as Madeleine was supposed to be by Carlotta's. The shadow materialising as a nun can stand as a symbol of Scottie's illumination: a far more satisfactory one than the Bhuddist monk who rescues Genjuro the potter from *his* dream-world in Mizoguchi's *Ugetsu Monogatari,* because her appearance corresponds to a development within Scottie's consciousness.

The film ends with the magnificent image of Scottie looking down from a great height to where Judy has fallen: magnificent, because it so perfectly crystallises our complexity of response. Scottie is cured: yet his cure has destroyed at a blow both the reality and the illusion of Judy/Madeleine, has made the *illusion* of Madeleine's death real. He is cured, but empty, desolate. Triumph and tragedy are indistinguishably fused.

* * *

Vertigo seems to me of all Hitchcock's films the one nearest to perfection. Indeed, its profundity is inseparable from the perfection of form: it is a perfect organism, each character, each sequence, each image, illuminating every other. Form and technique here become the perfect expression of concerns both deep and universal.

Hitchcock uses audience-involvement as an essential aspect of the film's significance. Together with its deeply disturbing attitude to life goes a strong feeling for the value of human relationships. To object that the characters' motives are not explained in terms of individual psychology is like demanding a psychological explanation of the sources of evil in Macbeth: Hitchcock is concerned with impulses that lie deeper than individual psychology, that are inherent in the human condition. The film's only blemish is the occasional inadequacy of Kim Novak as Judy. Her performance as Madeleine, lovingly moulded by Hitchcock, is flawless, but there are moments when one wants more inwardness from her Judy. The taxing long take of her composing the letter reveals this slight inadequacy: one becomes uncomfortably aware of the director behind the camera telling her "Now you do this . . . Now you do that . . ." But this weakness is not serious enough to detract from the poignancy of these last sequences. In complexity and subtlety, in emotional depth, in its power to disturb, in the centrality of its concerns, *Vertigo* can as well as any film be taken to represent the cinema's claims to be treated with the respect accorded to the longer-established art forms.

5. North by Northwest

> "There are no symbols in *North by Northwest*. Oh yes! One. The last shot. The train entering the tunnel after the love-scene between Grant and Eva-Marie Saint. It's a phallic symbol. But don't tell anyone". — HITCHCOCK, *Cahiers du Cinema* No. 102.

OF HITCHCOCK'S SIX most recent films, *North by Northwest* is that which corresponds most nearly to the conventional estimate of him as a polished light entertainer. That, beside its immediate neighbours, it is a lightweight work, a relaxation, in which we see Hitchcock working at something less than full pressure, I do not deny. That it is trivial or frivolous, not worth serious attention, I reject absolutely. When I spoke of the unbroken series of masterpieces from *Vertigo* to *Marnie,* I had not forgotten *North by Northwest.*

A light entertainment can have depth, subtlety, finesse, it can embody mature moral values; indeed, it seems to me that it *must.* If I fail to be entertained by *Goldfinger,* it is because there is nothing there to engage or retain the attention; the result is a nonentity, consequently tedious. The essential triviality of the James Bond films, in fact, sets off perfectly, by contrast, the depth, the charm, the integrity of Hitchcock's film.

A film, whether light entertainment or not, is either a work of art or it is nothing. And the basic essential of a work of art is that it be thematically organic. *Goldfinger* is a collection of bits, carefully calculated with both eyes on the box office, put end to end with no deeper necessity for what happens next than mere plot; nothing except plot develops in the course of it, and, obviously, the essence of an organic construction is development. But *Goldfinger,* I shall be reminded, doesn't take itself seriously: so much the worse for it. And if it doesn't why should anyone else? —for I find it difficult to see how the adult mind can occupy itself with something that cannot, in some sense, be taken seriously. *North by Northwest,* on the level of plot (if one can imagine its plot divorced from its subject, which is more difficult than may at first appear), also doesn't take itself seriously: we are not, in other words, expected to believe, literally, *this could happen.* But it is a very superficial glance that sees no more there than the plot. The tongue-in-cheek element on plot level has the function of directing our attention to other levels. On the other hand the self-mocking aspect of the Bond films is merely a very shrewd means of permitting the spectator to indulge any penchant for sadism and sexual "kicks" he may have without any accompanying discomfort.

The sociologist and the critic have territory in common, certainly; but *Goldfinger* and its success, the wide popular and critical success of a film that has scarcely more to offer than a boys' comic paper, seems to me to belong strictly to the sociologist. Even to compare it with

North by Northwest will seem slightly ridiculous to Hitchcock's admirers, but a moment's reflection will be enough to remind them that the obvious distinction between the two films has not been made everywhere.

I have allowed that *North by Northwest* is a comparatively relaxed film, a *divertissement;* that is to say, one must not demand of it the concentrated significance, the extraordinarily close-knit organisation of *Vertigo* and *Psycho.* Nevertheless, it has a coherent and satisfying development, a construction sufficiently strong and clear to assimilate the occasional charming but irrelevant little *jeux d'esprits* (the strange lady's reaction to Cary Grant's nocturnal passage through her bedroom as he escapes from the hotel in which the head of C.I.A. has imprisoned him) permissible in a work of this nature. Like *Vertigo* (to which it is also linked through its equivocal heroine), it can be regarded as falling into three movements corresponding to the main stages in the evolution of the hero's attitude. The first lightly sketches all that is relevant (for the purposes of the film) of his general situation and outlook, and has him mistaken for George Kaplan and wanted by both spies and police; it closes with the revelation that George Kaplan doesn't exist. The second sees him involved with Eve Kendall and traces the abrupt shifts in his relationship with her as he (as well as the spectator) becomes increasingly frustrated, baffled, disillusioned, by the ambiguity of her position and behaviour. The last movement begins when he learns the truth about her and—the real turning-point of the film—voluntarily accepts his role as Kaplan, and culminates in the cementing of their relationship.

North by Northwest bears an obvious resemblance to both *The 39 Steps* and *Saboteur;* its immense superiority to both films scarcely needs to be argued, but it is worth noting that Hitchcock himself, when asked why he had remade *Saboteur,* replied that in the earlier films the characters were not interesting, and that he made an elementary mistake in having the villain, not the hero, dangle from the top of the Statue of Liberty. The second point is by no means a trivial one, and is intimately connected with the first. It is not so much a greater complexity of the characters in *North by Northwest* that makes them more interesting, but their relationship to the action. Both *The 39 Steps* and *Saboteur* have heroes quite unpredictably and abruptly plunged into hair-raising adventures, but the adventures bear no really organic relationship to the men; there is not the same point in these things happening to Richard Hannay and the hero of *Saboteur* as there is in their happening to Roger Thornhill. Similarly, there is no point at all in having Fry (the "saboteur" of the title) hang by his coat-sleeves from the Statue of Liberty, beyond the prolonging of a simple suspense as an end in itself; there is every point in Roger Thornhill, the previously irresponsible, unattached advertising man, having to hang on to a ledge on Mount Rushmore by one hand, holding the woman he loves by the other, while the homosexual spy Leonard, the film's ultimate representative of the sterile and destructive, grinds the hand with his foot. The difference can be summed up (with some unfairness in simplification to the earlier films) by saying that *North by Northwest* has a subject as well as a plot.

In fact, at a deeper level the film has more in common with *Rear Window* than with *Saboteur* or *The 39 Steps*. The film begins with shots of New York traffic and New York crowds: a sense of apparently aimless and chaotic bustle and movement. From this emerges Roger Thornhill, dictating to his secretary on his way home by lift, crowded pavement, taxi: emerges from it as its typical representative and product. In an exposition of masterly compression we learn all the essential things about him: he is brash, fast-talking, over-confident on the surface; entirely irresponsible and inconsiderate of others (he cheats two people out of their taxi by pretending his secretary is ill, then cheerfully justifies this to her by telling her he has made the other man "feel like a Good Samaritan"); a heavy drinker; a divorcé (twice, it transpires); surprisingly dominated by his mother, who, he says, is "like a bloodhound" in still sniffing his breath to find out if he has been drinking. Indeed, he is a man who lives purely on the surface, refusing all commitment or responsibility (appropriately he is in advertising), immature for all his cocksureness, his life all the more a chaos for the fact that he doesn't recognise it as such; a man who relies above all on the exterior trappings of modern civilisation—business offices, cocktail bars, machines—for protection, who substitutes bustle and speed for a sense of direction or purpose: a modern city Everyman, whose charm and self-confidence and smartness make him especially easy for the spectator to identify with, so that at the start we are scarcely conscious of his limitations as a human being. We can quite happily and thoughtlessly attach ourselves to his smug confidence in being in control of his environment.

And then, abruptly, within ten minutes of the start of the film, the ground is cut away from under his/our feet. Hitchcock's sense of the precariousness of all human order has never been more beautifully expressed (though conveyed elsewhere—in *The Wrong Man* and *The Birds,* for instance—with greater intensity and overt seriousness) than in the mistake, due to sheer chance, by which Thornhill, going to send a telegram to his mother, finds himself kidnapped by gunmen. In the lobby of a crowded hotel, in whose lounge bar he has just been drinking with associates, chaos abruptly takes over.

The remainder of the film's first movement is devoted to a systematic stripping away of all the protective armour of modern city man on which Thornhill relies for his safety. In the midst of crowds, he becomes completely isolated. The opportunist has been defeated by chance. The man who deprived others of their taxi is imprisoned in a car he can't get out of, unable even to attract attention. He is taken to the house of a Mr. Townsend where all his "proofs" of identity are disdainfully refused. The heavy drinker is forced to gulp down immense quantities of Bourbon as a preliminary to a "drunk driving accident". The fact that he is a heavy drinker, of course, makes it

110

feasible that he should be able to frustrate his potential murderers by escaping his "accident"; but we are also left to reflect on the appropriateness of such a death—it is precisely the way in which Thornhill might eventually have died. The hair-raising drive in a car almost out of his control is a logical extension of his basic situation. And Hitchcock is so little interested in his spies *as* spies, the spectator is so little encouraged to inquire into the precise nature of their activities, that it becomes very easy to accept them as simply the embodiment of the forces of disorder and subversion: we are no more interested in their rational motivation than we are in that of the birds two films later. Like the birds, they are not so much a projection of the chaos underlying modern order as the agents whereby that order is destroyed, the chaos forced upon the characters' consciousness.

Thornhill's sense of personal identity is clearly weak, and undermined by the spies' unshakable conviction that he is George Kaplan; and indeed as an integrated human being he has about as real an existence. At the police station, he tells his mother on the 'phone, very emphatically, "This is your son, Roger Thornhill"—as if he had been brought to the point of doubting it. The only relationship of any apparent strength, with his mother, proves worse than useless, her scepticism undermining him at every step; it is parodied when he returns with the police to the Townsend mansion by the false Mrs. Townsend's effusive, motherly, yet equally cynical, treatment of him. The parallel is emphasized by Hitchcock's having the two women (who look very alike) stand in similar postures, hands folded before them. One of the film's funniest and most uncomfortable moments comes when, descending from their exploration of Kaplan's rooms in the hotel lift, Thornhill's mother remarks gaily to the two men who almost sent her son over a cliff the night before, "You gentlemen aren't *really* trying to kill my son, are you?", and the whole liftload—mother, killers, other passengers—laugh uproariously at the joke while Thornhill stands helplessly in their midst.

111

With characteristic Hitchcockian outrageousness, Thornhill's final plunge into chaos is set in the supreme symbol of potential world order, the United Nations building. After the knifing of the real Townsend, we see Thornhill running frantically, a microscopic figure, in a shot taken from the top of the building, looking directly down on him: the smug, self-confident advertising man, so sure of the effectiveness of his personality, reduced to an almost indistinguishable speck, and a completely isolated speck, for he is now (as Thornhill) pursued by the forces of order as well as of disorder (as Kaplan). It is at this point that we leave him for a moment to learn the truth: the meeting in the Intelligence Bureau reveals that Kaplan (on whose whereabouts Thornhill's fate depends) doesn't exist—is a convenient invention, a "non-existent decoy" designed to divert the spies' attention from the *real* agent. What is to be done to protect Thornhill? Nothing. He is to be left to fend for himself, thrown back on his own resources, all civilised protections removed. The first movement of the film ends with the secretary's epitaph on an unknown nonentity: "Good-bye, Mr. Thornhill, whoever you are!"

The second movement begins with Thornhill, in the station, again among crowds, into which we see him, in long-shot, disappear. The ensuing sequence gives us the train journey, Thornhill's meeting with Eve Kendall, and the first stage in their relationship. The superficial Eve—it is all we see for some time—suggests that she is the perfect counterpart for Thornhill: worldly, amoral, quite without depth of feeling, quite uncommitted to anything or anyone, taking sex as she would a cocktail (she says to him, with a sly suggestiveness, "It's going to be a long night, and I don't particularly like the book I've started . . . know what I mean?"). There is a slight hint of nymphomania. She seems to be offering exactly the kind of relationship he would want: love-making without involvement, sex without responsibilities. But already, as they begin to make love after she has hidden him in her wall bed from the searching police, one begins to be aware

NORTH BY NORTHWEST: top, "You gentlemen aren't really trying to kill my son, are you?"; and bottom, Grant: "Shall I?" Saint: "Please do."

of undercurrents. He wonders why she isn't afraid of him, a supposed murderer; she asks him if he is planning to murder her. He asks, "Shall I?"; she murmurs "Please do", and they kiss. It is all playful on the surface; but as they kiss his hands encircle her head as if either to strangle or to crush her, and hers move to his to draw him down, in an attitude of surrender. We realise his sudden sense of the danger of involvement and also her barely concealed weariness and yearning. It is all done with a marvellous delicacy which is in fact profoundly characteristic of Hitchcock, although this is not often recognised. The scene ends with a shot of her looking over his shoulder, her eyes deeply troubled; then she sends the message along to Vandamm: "What do I do with him in the morning?"

What she does is to arrange for him to be machine-gunned from a 'plane. The attempt on his life is prefaced by their parting, which ends with the beautiful shot of his hand tentatively covering hers on the handle of her case, as she draws back: their mutual involvement is suggested with remarkable economy. What we seem to have here (for we still take Eve very largely at her face-value) is the old cliché of the wicked woman drawn into true love against her will. A cursory comparison with what Guy Hamilton makes of the Pussy Galore/James Bond relationship will reveal the extent to which a "light entertainment" can have grace, sensibility and moral depth if it is directed by Hitchcock.

The crop-dusting sequence is justly famous and seems widely accepted as one of Hitchcock's most brilliant set-pieces. What is not so often noticed, however, is its dependence for much of its effect on its context. Certainly, it is brilliant in itself, an object-lesson in the building up of suspense through the repeated cheating of the audience's expectations, ending in the *frisson*-producing line, "That plane's dusting crops where there ain't no crops", and the subsequent explosion into violent action. Yet the sequence retains its magic however many times one sees the film— even after one knows, shot by shot, what comes next, and

114

it is worth asking why this should be. The sequence occurs at almost exactly midpoint in the film. Immediately behind it is our knowledge of Eve Kendall's treachery (*we* know Thornhill is going to be attacked, though *he* doesn't) and all the emotional tension generated by their relationship. But there is much more behind it than that. Hitherto in the film, Thornhill has always been *inside:* inside cities, buildings, vehicles: and we know him as a man at home in the complacency-encouraging security of office and cocktail-bar. Now, suddenly, he is in open country. And not merely open country: a flat landscape, treeless, house-less, shelterless, parched, stretching away apparently to infinity on all sides. In the midst of this he stands, an iso-lated speck with the whole world against him, absolutely exposed and vulnerable: modern man deprived of all his amenities and artificial resources. The bus—his last con-tact with other people, with civilisation—moves away, the crop-dusting plane turns and flies towards him . . . It is a marvellous conception, central to the film in more ways than position.

Thornhill's first image of Eve is now shattered; the second is equally misleading—though both bear some relationship to the real Eve. When they meet again in the hotel, she runs up to him, and we see her relief: relief not only that he isn't dead but that she hasn't been re-sponsible for his death. His hands go round her head again to embrace her, in the gesture he used on the train; only this time they don't quite touch. He hesitates, moves away, makes a sarcastic remark about "togetherness". Another familiar Hitchcock theme is touched on: the necessity for a trust based on instinct, even when it is quite unreasonable. Their separation is expressed by restless cross-cutting, their partial reconciliation (on his side clearly provisional and suspicious) by a beautiful camera-movement that unites them in one image as she moves towards him. She helps him remove his jacket to have it cleaned, and he says, "When I was a little boy I wouldn't even let my mother undress me"; she tells him he is a big boy now. It is one of those unobtrusive, almost off-hand exchanges that reveals a great deal. Before she leaves, he asks her, "Have you ever killed anyone?"—we are made to remember that (whatever her motives) she did in fact connive at the attempt on his life.

This middle movement of the film closes with the auction scene, which gives us Thornhill's view of Eve at its most bitterly disillusioned ebb. Vandamm is standing behind her, his hand closing round the back of her neck in what constitutes at once a caress and a threat. A close-up emphasises this, and we connect it with Thornhill's embraces, but this is far more sinister, and expresses the precariousness of Eve's position (before we know the truth about her). Thornhill calls her a "statue" and tells her: "Who are you kidding? You *have* no feelings to hurt". We see, but he doesn't, that she is in tears: the sequence is a condensed recapitulation of *Notorious*. This is not so banal as it sounds. We are aware by this time of the potentially healing power of the relationship on both sides (though we still don't know the real nature of Eve's need); but it appears—as Thornhill escapes thanks to the police—irremediably broken.

The final movement opens with the reversal of this situation. At the airport, the head of C.I.A. tells Thornhill the truth about Eve, and he accepts his role as Kaplan for her sake. Immediately before, he uses a phrase that unites his two images of her: "That treacherous little tramp". Suddenly he learns that her life may depend on him, and, in agreeing to be Kaplan, he is accepting his responsibility and his involvement in a deep relationship. The sexual basis of his previous refusal of commitment, rejection of responsibility, is clear: he has survived two marriages which have left him, apparently, completely unaffected. As he accepts, his face is suddenly illuminated by the light of the plane; and we cut to the first shot of Mount Rushmore. The cut has great emotional effect, because it abruptly defines for us, with marvellous economy, the evolution of the hero. For if the significance of Mount Rushmore is dramatic rather than symbolic, it is because "symbolic" suggests something too precise and

116

NORTH BY NORTHWEST:
towards "togetherness" (the guardians of order presiding in the background).

too simple. It is not a symbol of democracy standing against the wicked agents; but certainly, in its emotional effect, it suggests the order and stability towards which Thornhill is progressing, and to which the acceptance of a strong relationship with its accompanying responsibilities is the essential step.

The scene of his reconciliation with Eve (after the false shooting) is perhaps the most beautiful in the film. First, the location: for the first time in the film we are among trees, cool calm sunlight and shade—the effect is more a matter of context than of intrinsic beauty of the scenery, and (as usual in this film, indeed in all Hitchcock's work) more of overtones and associations than of overt, clear-cut symbolism; it is an apt setting for the beginning of new life. Second, the *mise-en-scène*. As the "dead" Thornhill gets out of the back of the car, the camera tracks back to reveal Eve standing by *her* car to the right. We see them in long shot gazing at each other from the extremities of the screen, across the space of trees and filtered sunlight, everything still, the two hesitant, as if shy of each other. Then a shot of Thornhill as he begins to move: the camera tracks with him, left to right. Cut to a shot of Eve as *she* starts forward: the camera tracks with her from right to left. And so they are united: Hitchcock beautifully involves the spectator in their movement towards each other, their movement towards the "togetherness" that was earlier (for Thornhill) a contemptuous sneer.

We, and Thornhill, see at last the real Eve; or perhaps it is truer to say that the real Eve now *emerges:* her true identity is created—or at least crystallised—by the relationship, superceding (or perhaps assimilating) her two earlier *personae*. But it is made clear that those earlier Eves, partly artificial, are what she could have become, just as the real Judy Barton contains elements of her two adopted "personalities" (in *Vertigo* the distinction between them is of course much greater). It is the real Eve who tells Thornhill, with a touching gentleness, how deeply his words hurt; but almost at once, we get a glimpse of the

118

first Eve, the Eve of the train journey, in her description of her relationship with Vandamm: "I had nothing to do that weekend, so I decided to fall in love". Then her comment on her decision to help Intelligence ("Maybe that was the first time anyone ever asked me to do anything worthwhile") gives us the potentially ruthless Eve—ruthless in a good cause—who could send Thornhill (with whatever qualms) to his death, and who is still ready to sacrifice their relationship for the "cause". The strands are drawn together in the ensuing dialogue exchange: "Has life been like that?" he asks her, and she assents. "How come?"—"Men like you!"—"What's wrong with men like me?"—"They don't believe in marriage". He tells her he's been married twice: her comment, "See what I mean?" Circumstances have steered her towards being one or other of the earlier Eves; now, in the relationship with Thornhill, her true self can be realised.

She makes it clear that this marriage is one, at last, that he will not easily escape. His reaction is jocular, cynical—"I may go back to hating you: it was more fun". His expression and tone belie the words, but they serve to bring before us the man's previous fear of real involvement, of responsibility. Hitchcock—here and in *Rear Window*—gives us no simple "redemption through love", no abrupt transformation; just a delicate intimation of the potential healing power of a balanced, permanent relationship. Eve reminds him that he is "meant to be critically wounded"; he replies, "I never felt more alive".

That charming father figure, the head of the C.I.A., whom Jean Douchet appears to suggest is some kind of Divine Instrument, seems to me to come out of things pretty badly. The film is surely solidly behind Thornhill in rejecting the use of a woman to "get people like Vandamm": prostitution, in however admirable a cause, remains prostitution. Mixed morality—the pursuing of a good end by conventionally immoral means like Mark Rutland's in *Marnie*—is justified by Hitchcock only as the outcome of powerful instinctive drives, of basically right feelings, not when it comes to cold calculation: justifiable,

119

therefore, only on the personal level, not on the political. We are entirely behind Thornhill, then, in his attempts to extricate Eve—in the determined positive action that results from his acceptance of personal responsibility.

Before the Mount Rushmore climax, we have Thornhill's attempts to rescue Eve from Vandamm's house, Vandamm's discovery of her true nature, and his plans to dispose of her over the sea. Leonard is built up here as the incarnation of destruction and negation. His motive is sexual jealousy—jealousy of Eve, his rival for Vandamm. He discloses the truth about Eve in a melodramatic, vindictive way, by "shooting" Vandamm with her blank-loaded revolver.

The climax is played out on and around the imperturbable stone faces of the Presidents, with their suggestion of stability and order forming a background to Thornhill's desperate struggle to save himself and Eve for life. As they dangle from a ledge by their hands, they discuss—with total absurdity on a naturalistic level—Thornhill's first two marriages: "My wives divorced me . . . I think they said I led too dull a life". The struggle for life against the destructive elements (the spies) is thus combined with the cementing of the relationship, the sealing off of the past. The joining of the lovers' hands derives some of its emotional and moral force from our view of it as the climax of a sequence of shots of their hands touching (to mark phases in the relationship) earlier: her sensuous caressing of his hand over the lunch table on the train, when she looked at "R.O.T." matchpacket; his pressure on her hand at Chicago station as they say good-bye, after she has arranged the "meeting" with Kaplan. Eventually, Thornhill is hanging by one hand, holding the dangling Eve by the other, a great abyss beneath them: final test of stamina, with everything staked on his powers of endurance and determination. Leonard stands above them; Thornhill's "Help! Help me!" is given great force. Then Leonard treads on Thornhill's hand. Thornhill survives the trial for long enough: Leonard is shot down. We see Thornhill pulling Eve to safety. An abrupt cut, but with overlapping dialogue, makes the action culminate in his pulling her up into bed on a train, as "Mrs. Thornhill"— a beautiful way of expressing the link between his survival of the ordeal and their relationship. The last shot is of a train entering a tunnel: the "phallic symbol" towards which the whole film has moved.

It will be objected that this account of *North by Northwest* makes it far too serious. But its charms, its deftness, the constant flow of invention, its humour and exhilaration, are there for all to see. All I have tried to do is adjust the balance: not to turn a light comedy into an unsmiling morality play, but to suggest why *North by Northwest* is such a very, very good light comedy.

6. Psycho

> ".............. function
> Is smother'd in surmise, and nothing is
> But what is not".
>
> *(Macbeth)*

> "But if you look at the matter from a theoretical point of view and ignore this question of degree you can very well say that we are all ill, i.e. neurotic; for the conditions required for symptom-formation are demonstrable also in normal persons".
> (Freud, *Introductory Lectures on Psycho-Analysis*)

> "You have to remember that *Psycho* is a film made with quite a sense of amusement on my part. To me it's a *fun* picture. The processes through which we take the audience, you see, it's rather like taking them through the haunted house at the fairground . . ."
> (HITCHCOCK, interview in *Movie* 6)

Psycho OPENS WITH a view of a city. The name of the city appears followed by a precise date and a precise time, as the camera swings over the rooftops and apartment blocks. It hesitates, seems to select, tracks in towards one particular block, hesitates again before all the windows, seems to select again, then takes us through one slightly open window into a darkened room. Arbitrary place, date and time, and now an apparently arbitrary window: the effect is of random selection: this

121

could be any place, any date, any time, any room: it could be *us*. The forward track into darkness inaugurates the progress of perhaps the most terrifying film ever made: we are to be taken forwards and downwards into the darkness of ourselves. *Psycho* begins with the normal and draws us steadily deeper and deeper into the abnormal; it opens by making us aware of time, and ends (except for the releasing final image) with a situation in which time (i.e. development) has ceased to exist.

The scene we witness between Marion Crane (Janet Leigh) and Sam Loomis (John Gavin), while carefully and convincingly particularized in terms of character and situation, is ordinary enough for us to accept it as representative of "normal" human behaviour. A leading theme emerges, unexceptional both in itself and in the way in which it is presented, though it subtly pervades the whole scene: the dominance of the past over the present. The lovers cannot marry because Sam has to pay his dead father's debts and his ex-wife's alimony; "respectable" meetings in Marion's home will be presided over by her (presumably) dead mother's portrait. From this "normal" hold of past on present, with its limiting, cramping effect on life (the essence of life being development), we shall be led gradually to a situation where present is entirely swallowed up by past, and life finally paralysed. That the lovers are meeting surreptitiously, doing things that must be concealed from the outer world, provides a further link (still within the bounds of normality) with Norman Bates. And in both cases the "secrets", normal and abnormal, are sexual in nature.

Everything is done to encourage the spectator to indentify with Marion. In the dispute between the lovers we naturally side with her: Sam's insistence on waiting until he can give her financial security annoys us, because it is the sort of boring mundane consideration we expect the romantic hero of a film to sweep aside, and we are very much drawn to Marion's readiness to accept things as they are for the sake of the relationship. This is in fact the first step in our complicity in the theft of the 40,000 dollars. It is Sam's fault that Marion steals the money, which has no importance for her. It is simply the means to an end: sex, not money, is the root of all evil. Indeed, the spectator's lust for money, played upon considerably in the early stages of the film, is aroused only to be swiftly and definitively "placed": the fate of the money, after the shower murder, becomes an entirely trivial matter, and Hitchcock by insisting on it evokes in us a strong revulsion.

Our moral resistance is skilfully undermined during the office scene. The man with the money—Cassidy—is a vulgar, drunken oaf; he has plenty more; his boast that he "buys off unhappiness", that his about-to-be-married "baby" has "never had an unhappy day", fills us with a sense of unfairness even as we realise how far his boast probably is from the truth: whatever he is, Cassidy does not strike us as a happy man.

The whole fabric of the film is interwoven with these parent-child references: even Marion's fellow office-girl has a prying mother, and Marion's room is decorated with family photographs which look down on her as she packs. Cassidy's relationship with his "baby" takes us a step into the abnormal, because it is highly suspect: she will probably be better without the 40,000 dollar house, which is clearly a symbol of her father's power over her. That Marion will also be better without it is a reflection we do not allow ourselves, any more than she does. By minimizing our moral opposition to the notion of stealing 40,000 dollars, Hitchcock makes it possible for us to continue to identify with Marion, involving ourselves in her guilt as easily and unthinkingly as she herself becomes involved. There is no clear-cut moment of decision: she takes the money home, changes, packs her suitcase, but the money lies on the bed and she constantly hesitates over it: her actions tell us that she has committed herself, but she doesn't consciously accept that commitment. We are able to commit acts we know to be immoral only if we inhibit our conscious processes: Macbeth never really knows why he *"yields* to that suggestion whose

123

horrid image does unfix his hair . . .", but the yielding itself involves the paralysis of his conscious moral faculties. So it is with Marion: the decision having gripped her (rather than been taken), she necessarily forfeits her powers of conscious will. She drifts helplessly, and we drift with her.

Her inability to control her actions rationally is illustrated in numerous incidents. As she drives, she imagines voices, conversations: Sam, her boss, Cassidy. She knows Sam will be horrified, will reject the money (she cannot finish the imaginary conversation with him); yet she drives on. Her boss notices her as her car is held up by traffic-lights, and she sees him notice her; yet she drives on. Everything she imagines stresses the impossibility of getting away with it and the uselessness of it anyway; yet she drives on. A suspicious policeman sees her changing cars, and she knows that *he* knows what her new car looks like, and what its number is, and that she is throwing away an irretrievable 700 dollars pointlessly; yet she goes through with the exchange. Throughout the journey Hitchcock uses every means to enforce audience-identification —the staging of each scene, the use of subjective technique, the way in which each subsidiary character is presented to us through Marion's eyes, Bernard Herrmann's music and Hitchcock's use of it, all serve to involve us in Marion's condition. With her, we lose all power of rational control, and discover how easily a "normal" person can lapse into a condition usually associated with neurosis. Like her we resent, with fear and impatience, everything (the policeman, the car salesman) that impedes or interferes with her obsessive flight, despite the fact that only interference can help her; just as, two films later, Marnie will be helped only by events that are entirely contrary to her wishes, everything she wants being harmful to her. As Marion drives on (after the exchange of cars) we share her hopelessness and her weariness. The film conveys a sense of endless journey leading nowhere, or into darkness: as the imagined voices become more menacing, darkness gathers. Driving through darkness,

PSYCHO: left, Marion (Janet Leigh) and the owner of the money (Frank Albertson); and right, Marion in the grip of compulsion.

she imagines Cassidy learning of the theft of the money: "I'll replace it with her fine soft flesh": Marion's verdict on herself, hideously disproportionate to the crime, will find its hideous enactment. Rain begins to fall on the windscreen before Marion—before us. She pulls up at the Bates Motel, which seems to materialise abruptly out of the darkness in front of her. She has by her actions penetrated the shell of order, and like Macbeth plunged herself into the chaos-world, which finds here its most terrifying definition.

The confrontation of Marion and Norman Bates (Anthony Perkins) is in some ways the core of the film: the parallel made between them provides the continuity that underlies the brutal disruption when Marion is murdered. It is part of the essence of the film to make us feel the continuity between the normal and the abnormal: between the compulsive behaviour of Marion and the psychotic behaviour of Norman Bates. In the "parlour" behind his office, surrounded by Norman's stuffed birds and paintings of classical rapes, they talk about "traps". Marion is brought face to face with the logical extension of her present condition. Norman tells her, "We're all in our private trap. We scratch and claw, but only at the air, only at each other, and for all of it we never budge an inch": he is defining the psychotic state, the condition of permanent anguish whence development becomes impossible, a psychological hell. The parallel between the two is clinched when Norman says to her, "We all go a little mad sometimes. Haven't you?"

It is her perception of Norman's condition that gives Marion her chance of salvation, which she takes. In answer to his question, she says, "Sometimes just one time can be enough. Thank you". She decides to return the money the next morning. The decision this time is clearly made: she has regained her freedom of will, her power of rationality. The scene prepares us for the transference of our interest from Marion to Norman. We see Marion under the shower, and her movements have an almost

126

PSYCHO: top, "The confrontation of Marion and Norman Bates (Anthony Perkins) is in some ways the core of the film"; and bottom, Norman in his "private trap."

ritualistic quality; her face expresses the relief of washing away her guilt.

It is not merely its incomparable physical impact that makes the shower-bath murder probably the most horrific incident in any fiction film. The *meaninglessness* of it (from Marion's point of view) completely undermines our recently restored sense of security. The murder is as irrational and as useless as the theft of the money. It also constitutes an alienation effect so shattering that (at a first viewing of the film) we scarcely recover from it. Never—not even in *Vertigo*—has identification been broken off so brutally. At the time, so engrossed are we in Marion, so secure in her potential salvation, that we can scarcely believe it is happening; when it is over, and she is dead, we are left shocked, with nothing to cling to, the apparent centre of the film entirely dissolved.

Needing a new centre, we attach ourselves to Norman Bates, the only other character (at this point) available. We have been carefully prepared for this shift of sympathies. For one thing, Norman is an intensely sympathetic character, sensitive, vulnerable, trapped by his devotion to his mother—a devotion, a self-sacrifice, which our society tends to regard as highly laudable. That he is very unbalanced merely serves to evoke our protective instincts: he is also so helpless. Beyond this, the whole film hitherto has led us to Norman, by making us identify with a condition in many ways analogous to his: the transition is easy. After the murder, Hitchcock uses all the resources of identification technique to make us "become" Norman. He is a likeable human being in an intolerable situation, desperately in need of help and protection yet by the very nature of the case unable to obtain it. As he cleans up after his mother's hideous crime, the camera becomes subjective; they are our hands mopping away the blood. At the same time we cannot forget Marion; the intense anguish aroused in the spectator arises, as usual, from a conflict of responses. Our attention is directed repeatedly to the last lingering trace of Marion which Norman almost overlooks: the money, become now a mere squalid bundle of paper, an ironic reminder of her life, her desires, her relationship with Sam.

Psycho is Hitchcock's ultimate achievement to date in the technique of audience-participation. In a sense, the spectator becomes the chief protagonist, uniting in himself all the characters. The remainder of the film is an inquiry into the sources of the psychological hell-state represented by Norman Bates: a descent into the chaos-world. The other characters (Sam, Lila, Arbogast), perfunctorily sketched, are merely projections of the spectators into the film, our instruments for the search, the easier to identify with as they have no detailed individual existence. Each stage in the descent adds to the tension within us: we want to know, and we dread knowing, we want the investigators to find the truth and put an end to the horrors, yet we have involved ourselves in those horrors through our identification with Norman. One is struck, (bearing in mind the care with which Hitchcock always selects his players) by close physical resemblances between certain characters. That between Vera Miles and Janet Leigh can be easily explained: they are sisters: but what of that, still more striking, between Anthony Perkins and John Gavin? As they face each other across the counter of Norman's office, we have the uncanny feeling that we are looking at two sides of the same coin; and the scene in question, which seemed at first mere suspense, useful only in its plot context, becomes one of the most moving of the film. The two men look at one another, and we look at them, and we realise suddenly that they are interchangeable: each seems the reflection of the other (though a reflection in a distorting mirror), the one healthy, balanced, the other gnawed and rotted within by poisoned sex. Similarly, Vera Miles is the extension of Janet Leigh, and what she sees is, potentially, inside herself. The characters of *Psycho* are *one* character, and that character, thanks to the identifications the film evokes, is us.

Lila's exploration of the house is an exploration of

129

Norman's psychotic personality. The whole sequence, with its discoveries in bedroom, attic and cellar, has clear Freudian overtones. The Victorian *décor,* crammed with invention, intensifies the atmosphere of sexual repression. The statue of a black cupid in the hall, the painting of an idealised maiden disporting herself at the top of the stairs, a nude goddess statuette in the bedroom, are juxtaposed with the bed permanently indented with the shape of Mrs. Bates's body (the bed in which, we learn later, she and her lover were murdered by Norman), the macabre cast of crossed hands on her dressing-table, the stifling atmosphere of stagnation: one can almost *smell* it. The attic, Norman's own bedroom, represents the sick man's conscious mental development: strange confusion of the childish and the adult, cuddly toys, grubby unmade bed, a record of the "Eroica" symphony; the unexplained nature of all this carries the suggestion that what we see are mere superficial hints of underlying mysteries, a suggestion confirmed by the clasped, untitled book that Lila never actually opens (a Bates family album?) Consequently we accept Norman more than ever as a human being, with all the human being's complex potentialities. The cellar gives us the hidden, sexual springs of his behaviour: there Lila finds Mrs. Bates. It is a *fruit*-cellar— the fruit is insisted upon in the mother's macabre joke about being "fruity": the source of fruition and fertility become rotten.

Our discovery of the truth, of course, partly changes our attitude to what has gone before. It adds, for example, many complexities to our understanding of the shower murder, which we see now as primarily a sexual act, a violent substitute for the rape that Norman dare not carry out, and secondarily as the trapped being's desire to destroy a woman who has achieved the freedom he will never achieve: a point that gives added irony to the fact that it is her awareness of Norman that gives Marion that freedom. What it cannot do is remove our sense of complicity. We have been led to accept Norman Bates as

130

a potential extension of ourselves. That we all carry within us somewhere every human potentiality, for good or evil, so that we all share in a common guilt, may be, intellectually, a truism; the greatness of *Psycho* lies in its ability, not merely to *tell* us this, but to make us experience it. It is this that makes a satisfactory analysis of a Hitchcock film on paper so difficult; it also ensures that no analysis, however detailed, can ever become a substitute for the film itself, since the direct emotional experience survives any amount of explanatory justification.

The effect of forward tracking-shots in the film (from the opening right through to Lila's exploration of the house) is to carry us always further inside or into darkness. All the time we are being made to *see,* to see more, to see deeper: often, to see things we are afraid to see. Hence the insistence on eyes, into which the camera, our own eyes, makes us look, to see the dark places of the human soul beyond. And hence the dark glasses of the policeman: he is the only character whose eyes we never see, because it is he who is watching Marion, and hence ourselves. By the end of the film, Hitchcock has placed us in the policeman's position: we watch Norman Bates as the policeman watched Marion, and he is as conscious of our gaze as Marion was of the policeman's. On the other side of the cinema screen, we are as inscrutable, hence as pitiless, as the policeman behind his dark glasses. We may recall Norman's remark about "institutions" in the dialogue with Marion: ". . . the cruel eyes studying you". Norman is finally beyond our help. Much of the film's significance is summed up in a single visual metaphor, making use again of eyes, occurring at the film's focal point (the murder of Marion): the astonishing cut from the close-up of the water and blood *spiralling* down the drain, to the close-up of the eye of the dead girl, with the camera *spiralling* outwards from it. It is as if we have emerged from the depths *behind* the eye, the round hole of the drain leading down into an apparently bottomless darkness, the potentialities for horror that lie in the depths

131

of us all, and which have their source in sex, which the remainder of the film is devoted to sounding. The sensation of vertigo inspired by this cut and the spiralling movement itself, are echoed later as we, from high above, watch Norman carry his mother down to the fruit cellar.

The cellar is another clear sex symbol. And what Vera Miles finds there at the end of the quest are once again eyes: the mocking "eyes" of a long-dead corpse as a light-bulb swings before its face: the eyes of living death, eyes that move without seeing, the true eyes of Norman.

The psychiatrist's "explanation" has been much criticized, but it has its function. It crystallises for us our tendency to evade the implications of the film, by converting Norman into a mere "case", hence something we can easily put from us. The psychiatrist, glib and complacent, reassures us. But Hitchcock crystallises this for us merely to force us to reject it. We shall see on reflection that the "explanation" ignores as much as it explains (the murder as symbolic rape, for example). But we are not allowed to wait for a chance to reflect: our vague feelings of dissatisfaction are promptly brought to consciousness by our final confrontation with Norman, and this scene in the cell, entirely static after the extremes of violence that have preceded it, is the most unbearably horrible in the film. What we see is Norman, his identity finally dissolved in the illusory identity of his mother, denounce all the positive side of his personality. "Mother" is innocent: "she" spares the fly crawling on Norman's hand: it is Norman who was the savage butcher. Thus we witness the irretrievable annihilation of a human being. The fly reminds us of Marion, who wasn't spared: the act constitutes a pathetic attempt at expiation before the pitiless eyes of a cruel and uncomprehending society. For a split second, almost subliminally, the features of the mother's ten-year-dead face are superimposed on Norman's as it fixes in a skull-like grimace. The sense of finality is intolerable, yet it is this that makes our release possible: we have been made to see the dark potentialities within all of us, to face the worst thing in the world: eternal damnation. We can now be set free, be saved for life. The last image, of the car *withdrawing* from the dark depths of the bog, returns us to Marion, to ourselves, and to the idea of psychological liberty.

* * *

Psycho is one of the key works of our age. Its themes are of course not new—obvious forerunners include *Macbeth* and Conrad's *Heart of Darkness*—but the intensity and horror of their treatment and the fact that they are here grounded in sex belong to the age that has witnessed on the one hand the discoveries of Freudian psychology and on the other the Nazi concentration camps. I do not think I am being callous in citing the camps in relation to a work of popular entertainment. Hitchcock himself in fact accepted a commission to make a compilation film of captured Nazi material about the camps. The project reached the rough-cut stage, and was abandoned there, for reasons I have not been able to discover: the rough-cut now lies, inaccessibly, along with vast quantities of similar raw material, in the vaults of the Imperial War Museum. But one cannot contemplate the camps without confronting two aspects of their horror: the utter helplessness and innocence of the victims, and the fact that human beings, whose potentialities all of us in some measure share, were their tormentors and butchers. We can no longer be under the slightest illusion about human nature, and about the abysses around us and within us; and *Psycho* is founded on, precisely, these twin horrors. For Hitchcock it was a "fun" picture, and a streak of macabre humour ("Mother . . . what is the phrase? . . . isn't quite herself today") certainly runs through it. Is it, then, some monstrous perversion? Many have found it so, and their reaction seems to me more defensible than that of those (must we include Hitchcock himself?) who are merely amused by it (". . . make us think twice about stopping at any building looking remotely like the Bates motel . . ."). David Holbrook, for example, remarks (presumably with *Psycho* in mind, since his book appeared in 1962), "Of course, if we live in the world of detective stories and Hitchcock films we may take all this sordidness in a light-hearted spirit as a snuff-like piece of stimulation. But if we are responding to poetry and drama our senses should be sharpened . . ." *(Llareggub Revisited).* Yet this seems to me a short-sighted and insensitive verdict: if one is responding to *Psycho,* one's senses should be sharpened too. No film conveys—to those not afraid to expose themselves fully to it—a greater sense of desolation, yet it does so from an exceptionally mature and secure emotional viewpoint. And an essential part of this viewpoint is the detached sardonic humour. It enables the film to contemplate the ultimate horrors without hysteria, with a poised, almost serene detachment. This is probably not what Hitchcock meant when he said that one cannot appreciate *Psycho* without a sense of humour, but it is what he *should* have meant. He himself—if his interviews are to be trusted—has not really faced up to what he was doing when he made the film. This, needless to say, must not affect one's estimate of the film itself. For the maker of *Psycho* to regard it as a "fun" picture can be taken as his means of preserving his sanity; for the critic to do so—and to give it his approval on these grounds—is quite unpardonable. Hitchcock (again, if his interviews are to be trusted) is a much greater artist than he knows.

7. The Birds

MY OWN EXPERIENCE with *The Birds* has been varied and disconcerting. At first it seemed to me a great disappointment; now, after repeated viewings, it seems to me among Hitchcock's finest achievements. Talking oneself round to the point of view one wishes to hold is a not uncommon phenomenon, and for a time I distrusted my own deepening response to the film for this reason. But I don't think my experience of *The Birds* has been of this kind: rather, it has been a matter of breaking down a number of misleading preconceptions, so that only at the fifth or sixth viewing did I feel that I was really seeing the film, instead of being frustrated because it wasn't what I had assumed it was going to be and ought to have been; only then did it begin to make complete, instead of merely fragmentary and intermittent, sense.

For those who come to it with Hitchcock's preceding films—and especially *Psycho*—fresh in their minds, *The Birds* raises in particular two major red herrings: 1. The mother-son relationship, which leads one off the track into speculation about possessive-incestuous involvement, despite Hitchcock's explicit warning (through Annie Hayworth) that Lydia is not a "jealous, possessive mother" (a diagnosis amply confirmed later in the film in the development of Lydia herself). 2. The rather tentative use of those audience-identification techniques familiar from *Vertigo* and *Psycho* to involve us with Melanie Daniels in certain parts of the film. This can lead us to feel that we are being asked to *be* Melanie as in the first part of *Psycho* we were Marion Crane, and if we approach the film with this preconception it can seem only a disastrous failure. In fact, the identification Hitchcock encourages in *The Birds* is of a far more delicate and intermittent nature: the method of the film is quite unlike that of *Psycho,* both in the *mise-en-scène* and in the construction of the scenario. These errors of approach arise from too simple a notion of an artist's line of development, which rarely takes the form of such a straightforward extension of theme and technique from film to film.

Certain visual reminiscences from *Psycho* can also be misleading, though less drastically. Melanie's ascent of the stairs to her near-death in the upper room it treated in a manner recalling that of Lila Crane's exploration of the Bates house; and the birds' actual assault on Melanie carries strong reminders of the shower-bath murder. Neither of these parallels is of any *direct* help in reaching the core of the film. Melanie is much more than an audience projection *à la* Lila, and she is not used as our instrument for 'discovering what is up there', since we already guess; and Melanie's agony has a significance quite different from Marion's. Yet if there *is* a clue to *The Birds* in *Psycho,* it is certainly the shower murder, and it is not irrelevant to recall that Norman Bates, when carrying out his murders, becomes a bird of prey.

Then there are the birds themselves: what do they mean? everyone wants to know; or why do they attack? 1. *The birds are taking revenge for man's persecution of them.* Hitchcock is at pains to encourage this view in his rather lamentable misfire of a trailer. In fact, one neither accepts nor rejects it: it does so little towards explaining the film as to appear merely irrelevant. 2. *They are sent by God to punish evil humanity.* Scarcely, unless we postulate an unusually monstrous and callous God: an Old Testament God, not a Christian one: the indiscriminate nature of the attacks is the stumbling-block to a theory one is quick to reject as quite foreign to the tone and temper of the film. 3. *The birds express the tensions between the characters.* This is more interesting, and seems to gain some support when one considers the original attack on Melanie by the seagull. But objections soon pile up: the birds attack innocent schoolchildren and kill Dan Fawcett, of whose possible tensions we know nothing.

The film itself is quite insistent that either the birds can't be explained or that the explanation is unknown; and it seems reasonable to start from this. Consider the totally arbitrary and pointless nature of the shower murder in *Psycho* from the point of view of Marion and her development at that point. From her point of view—which is after all that from which we have been watching the film—the murder has no dramatic, symbolic, or thematic justification. If she were still in her compulsive state, if she had not just been released from it and made her free decision to return the money, the murder could be taken as having some validity as retribution (though grossly disproportionate), or as a symbolic representation of the irrevocability of her descent into the chaos-world. But Marion is saved. It is partly because the murder is—

136

again, from her point of view—entirely arbitrary and unpredictable that its effect is so shattering. We are made to feel at that moment the precariousness, the utter unreasonableness, of life.

This disturbing sense of precariousness, of unpredictability, is of course very common in Hitchcock, who delights in disrupting a normal, everyday atmosphere with some alarming event. But usually, hitherto, the event has some justification. If Guy Haines meets Bruno Anthony, it is because something of Bruno exists already in him; if Ben and Jo *(The Man Who Knew Too Much)* get involved with spies, it is because, in the near-stalemate of their marriage, they crave some external excitement; if Roger Thornhill is mistaken for Kaplan, the disorder of his life makes the mistake appropriate. But the murder of Marion Crane is in no way and to no extent either provoked or deserved.

And this seems to me the function of the birds: they are a concrete embodiment of the arbitrary and unpredictable, of whatever makes human life and human relationships precarious, a reminder of fragility and instability that cannot be ignored or evaded and, beyond that, of the possibility that life is meaningless and absurd. Hitchcock said that his film was about "complacency".

* * *

The opening shots of the film, as so often in Hitchcock, state the theme with almost diagrammatic simplicity. Melanie Daniels (Tippi Hedren) crosses a street in San Francisco; overhead, birds mass in ominous dark clouds. She enters an expensive pet shop; she is surrounded by birds in ornamental cages. Outside, reality, with its constant menace of instability; inside, the 'safe' artificial world that sophisticated human beings fabricate and call reality. The light comedy of the opening sequence is not merely there to lull the spectator into a state of unpreparedness for the coming horrors. The triviality is the point: the triviality of constant, even habitual play-acting. Indeed

137

the essential point about Melanie is revealed (with characteristic lack of fuss) before she even enters the shop: the determined elegance, which is very close to awkwardness, of her walk, gives us a girl whose sophistication is a disguise for underlying insecurity; she is whistled at, and turns with a smile of enjoyment at once self-conscious and childish, welcoming any boost, however vain, to her ego; then she promptly looks up, uneasily, at the birds flocking far overhead. The point is made explicit by Mitch Brenner's 'parallel' as he slips the canary back into the cage: Melanie is imprisoned in a gilded cage of sophisticated triviality, an inability to be sincere which is an inability to live. We see that she is both exasperated and attracted by Brenner (Rod Taylor): her practical joke is motivated by contradictory impulses—to make a fool of him and to be mastered by him.

The 'parallel' is developed in the ensuing scenes. As Melanie stands in the lift taking the love-birds to Brenner's apartment, the camera (following the gaze of the fellow-occupant) moves up from her legs and the hand holding the bird-cage to her face, and we see that, in her tense and affected stance, head cocked self-consciously on one side, she is curiously bird-like. Her behavior and her attitude, like the stance, are unnatural and dehumanizing—life rendered insignificant in the gilded cage of artificiality.

But such reflections scarcely occur to us at this stage of the film, where the tone is of brittle comedy, Melanie's behaviour, like the girl herself, seems cute and smart, we respond with an indulgent smile. It is later developments that condemn, retrospectively, her behaviour, our response, and the tone itself; for brittle comedy is based on the assumption that relationships don't really matter, and are a kind of game we play until we are bored. In retrospect, then, these opening sequences assume serious overtones already, and Melanie, instead of seeming cute, seems already pathetic.

The drive to Bodega Bay has superficial affinities with Marion's drive in *Psycho:* both girls seem trapped in a pattern of behaviour from which they cannot extricate themselves, and which they cannot view objectively, each successive step involving them in it more deeply. But the treatment, defining the spectator's relationship to the action, is completely different. When Marion was driving, we were restricted almost exclusively to her vision and her emotions; in *The Birds* we cut from a forward-moving close-up of Melanie (with ugly back-projection) to a vast static view of the landscape from high above. Identification, in other words, is not insisted upon. *The Birds* is far more 'open' than *Psycho:* we are at liberty to respond in different ways. Though our indulgence is invited by the light tone of the film so far, we are free to be critical of Melanie if we wish. We are also free, therefore, to contemplate her behaviour and ponder her motives, as we were not free to contemplate Marion. And we find ourselves in a state of extreme uncertainty. Are we watching a completely fatuous and pointless game? Just what is the delivery of the love-birds meant to achieve? On the conscious level, there seems no satisfactory answer: going to endless trouble to perform a service seems a peculiar way to avenge an insult. We are left to conclude that Melanie knows why she is doing it even less than we do. Clearly she can't leave Mitch Brenner alone: he constitutes a challenge, though of what sort we can't yet say. All that is clear is that she is giving him something, and something that he associates with her, that is even for him a symbol of her: birds in a gilded cage. We deduce, then, a split between supposed motives and true motives. Consciously, she is playing a silly, trivial trick (the birds, we learn later, were to be accompanied by a 'smart' note hoping that love-birds will "do something" for Brenner's personality); subconsciously, she is trying to continue the relationship and provoke further developments; perhaps to show him she is a nice girl after all; perhaps even to offer herself to him (to his masculine protection?) symbolically. This concealment—or, on a conscious level, rejection—of deep needs beneath a deliberately cultivated shallowness is the essential theme of these opening sequences.

It is during the sequence of the delivery of the lovebirds by boat that deliberate identification-techniques are most in evidence: though again, much less consistently than in *Psycho*. Before this, our sympathy for Melanie has been carefully increased. We see her charm the kindly old storekeeper, whose warmth and natural directness makes a strong contrast with the maddening fussiness and insincerity of the manageress of the bird-shop. Journeys in Hitchcock's films always represent more than a method of getting a character from place to place: Melanie has progressed in behaviour since we saw her in San Francisco, and the change of background reflects something of this development: she is slightly less tense, her inner concern is rising nearer the surface. Like the old man, we admire her determination and efficiency. We note her anxiety when the old man talks of 'the Brenners' and her relief when she learns that Mrs. Brenner is Mitch's mother, not his wife. She seems to be allowing herself to understand more of her motives. We are sufficiently softened not to rebel against being invited to be her temporarily as she leaves the love-birds and makes the return journey—an invitation made through the now familiar means of subjective shots and camera-movements.

Even here, however, the tendency to identification is offset by certain endistancing effects. During the journey across to the Brenners' landing-stage we are made to look *at* Melanie, not with her. For the close-ups and medium-shots back-projection is used again, as in the car journey. Arguments along these lines are admittedly dubious, but there seems some evidence to suggest that the use of back-projection in *The Birds* is a matter of deliberate choice rather than of mere convenience: there are several perfectly straightforward shots in the middle of sequences clearly made on location where back-projection is used, and they are always shots of Melanie. Whether intentional or not, it certainly has the effect of giving an air of unreality to her situation, of isolating her from the back-

140

grounds, of stressing her artificiality by making it stand out obtrusively from natural scenery. These close-ups are interspersed with long-shots that give us Melanie isolated, a tiny, defenceless figure in a vast open space. Behind her, flocks of gulls bob on the water. Advance publicity apart, the title of the film, the nerve-jangling credit-sequence, the birds massing over San Francisco, all warn us that there is going to be trouble from birds, and we expect Melanie to be attacked at any moment: they have her in a peculiarly vulnerable situation. This makes it impossible to identify with her completely as she delivers her present: we *are* expecting birds to attack, but she isn't. If we share with her something of her amusement at a joke that is becoming increasingly positive in its tendency (she tears up the letter to Mitch, substitutes one to Cathy), and share too her tension in case something goes wrong, she gets caught and made a fool of, we feel at the same time a deeper tension that she doesn't feel, as of something ominous and terrible hanging over these harmless proceedings, putting them in a different, disturbing perspective.

Melanie waits for Mitch to find the love-birds, and we watch with her. We see him come out, look around, see her, raise field-glasses to his eyes. She grins, bobs quickly down in the boat; Mitch grins too: she has got him, he is responding, we see him run to his car. But again Hitchcock clouds our amusement and deliberately interferes with our involvement: just before we see Mitch's response, the tranquillity of the shot is disrupted by seagulls abruptly fluttering and squawking across the foreground of the image: we think for a second that the attacks are beginning. There follows the race back to Bodega Bay— Melanie in the boat, Mitch in his car—and again any sense of exhilaration is clouded over by an anxiety not shared by the characters: she is out in the open again, far from help, exposed. But she reaches the other side, switches off the motor, drifts towards the jetty, timing her arrival beautifully to coincide with Mitch's. Both are pleased—indeed, delighted—and, as Melanie now seems safe, we relax to enjoy the reunion. But Melanie (annoy-

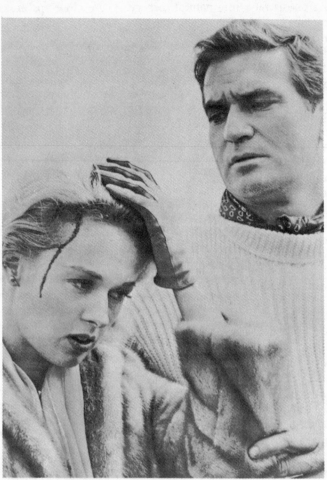

THE BIRDS: Melanie after the seagull's attack.

ingly? amusingly?) must go back to playing with him: she puts on an affected, coquettishly aloof expression, head on one side, suddenly bird-like again—and a seagull, hovering over her, abruptly swoops and pecks her head, drawing blood.

There are two ways in which Hitchcock could have made this sequence. Melanie could have been made more completely sympathetic, the reminders of her exposed isolation and of potential menace could have been eliminated, and we could have been led to become completely identified with her and her attitude; the seagull's attack would in this case have been aimed directly at us. Or her irritatingness and affectation could have been emphasized, the reminders of possible danger strengthened, and no identification set up by technical means; the attack would then have expressed *our* exasperation at her. In the event, Hitchcock rejects both methods; or combines them, if we prefer: it amounts to the same thing, in effect. Quite contradictory impulses are set up in the spectator. Hitchcock here is undertaking something more delicate and difficult to realise than the direct identification demanded by *Psycho:* the precise controlling of a partial and intermittent response to Melanie's attitudes, balanced by a sense of their insufficiency. We identify with Melanie enough to understand her, and enough to become aware of our own proneness to admire the sort of smart 'cleverness', with its trivialising effect on relationships, that she represents. Instead of encouraging a deep involvement that the spectator will only later be able to judge, Hitchcock here makes involvement and judgment virtually simultaneous.

Also, the two possible treatments I have suggested would give the seagull's attack too simple a significance. Although there is some appropriateness (derived from Melanie's atttude) in the attack occurring at that moment, there have been plenty of preceding moments when it would be just as appropriate. The birds are not a straightforward *punishment* for complacency; they are not *sent* to break down the characters' attitude so as to enable them to form relationships—nothing so schematic or explicable.

143

Indeed, we have been led to believe (despite Melanie's moment of affected aloofness) that the two were on the point of manoeuvring towards a viable relationship. Melanie is neither admirable nor contemptible; nothing in her behaviour could be dignified with the name 'evil'. And if all Hitchcock were after were a straightforward breaking down of a woman's complacency, he could have found characters in whom complacency was far more deeply embedded than in the obviously precariously balanced and vulnerable Melanie Daniels. If the film were simply the deliberate destruction of Melanie by the birds it would be unpardonably sadistic, the systematic torture of a child, the punishment monstrously disproportionate to any discernible crime. But the disproportion is at least part of the point: what happens to Melanie is neither the chastisement of the guilty nor the martyrdom of the innocent, for she is very carefully depicted as neither. The question we are left with, "What do you suppose made it (the seagull) do that?", is not meant to have an answer.

The ensuing scene in the café introduces Mrs. Brenner and certain parallels between the women that afford clues to an understanding of the film. Verbal parallels—and the common attitudes they express—link Mrs. Brenner and Annie Hayworth. The earlier scene, when Melanie visited Annie to learn Cathy Brenner's name, ended with Annie enquiring about the birds and, on learning that they were love-birds, exclaiming with an air of significance, "Oh, I see". The café scene ends almost identically, only this time the query and the significant "Oh, I see" are given to Lydia (Jessica Tandy). The link tells us for the moment only that both women regard Melanie's relationship with Mitch with anxious concern, perhaps jealousy. What matters at this stage is that the two women be linked in our minds, so that we retain the sense of a *thematic* connection between them. A visual parallel, on the other hand, links Lydia and Melanie: quite simply, the fact that they look remarkably alike, with the same shaped faces and very similar upswept hairstyles: almost, we feel, we are seeing Melanie as she will look in thirty

144

years' time. Hitchcock also supplies an almost subliminal link between Melanie and Annie, by having both women speak at moments with a similar intonation. These links are the more important in that in *personality* the three women are very strongly contrasted. Hitchcock is pointing to connections that lie deeper than personality, connections that link the three in terms of the human condition itself.

The introduction of Cathy when Melanie goes for dinner at the Brenners' puts the pattern of relationship in a slightly new perspective. Cathy rushes up to Melanie and hugs her, as soon as she has ascertained who she is, in gratitude for the love-birds; she is rebuked by her mother for referring to Mitch's San Francisco acquaintances (he is a lawyer) as "hoods", but continues to insist that that is what they are and everyone knows it; and when Melanie declines to stay for her birthday party, she asks right out, "Don't you like us?" Where the adults are circuitous and evasive, the child is direct. The child accepts Melanie at once as she is now, without question; Lydia and Mitch—to different degrees and from different viewpoints—hold her past against her. Relationships are easy for the child because they are uncomplicated by considerations other than intuitive like or dislike; the adults' relationships are constantly arrested or threatened by habitual attitudes. As Mitch sees Melanie off, telling her he'd like to see her again, they immediately fall into just such habitual attitudes, she adopting her smart aggressive-defensive manner, he leaning on the car door as if on the witness-box, cross-examining her.

Melanie's conversation with Annie when she gets back clarifies the pattern that is now emerging. Annie was and still is (as we and Melanie have guessed) in love with Mitch; their relationship was broken up by Lydia, whose husband had just died. Through Annie, Hitchcock makes it clear that what he is after is not the analysis of an Oedipus problem: "She's not afraid of losing Mitch", Annie tells Melanie, "She's afraid of being abandoned". She goes on to say that she herself came to Bodega Bay

145

to be near Mitch after it was all over. We see Annie's living-room, the room of a cultured woman (reproductions of Braque; long-playing records of Wagner), and we have seen something of Bodega Bay: we see how isolated her life must be and recall our introduction to her, coming round from her garden, describing her "tilling of the soil" as "compulsive". The point of the earlier suggestion of a link between her and Lydia now becomes clear: Annie too is "afraid of being abandoned"; she can't face the truth that she lost Mitch long ago—her behaviour towards Melanie suggests a whole fantasy-world of fulfilled love that reminds us strongly of the heroine of *I Confess,* a suggestion intensified by the records of *Tristan und Isolde* prominent in the décor. Although she is certainly "afraid of losing Mitch", or of having to admit she has lost him, it is her isolation that is insisted on. The hopelessness of her position is conveyed by one tiny movement—the closing of her eyes as Melanie, talking on the telephone to Mitch, agrees to stay for Cathy's party. With isolation becoming such a prominent theme, we think back to other images of isolation: Melanie alone in the bay with the birds on the water behind her: and to the very tentative and brittle nature of her relationship with Mitch. At the end of her telephone conversation she says to Annie, "Oh, it seems so pointless!" She asks Annie if she should go, and Annie tells her to—gives her permission to develop her relationship with Mitch. A bird thuds into the front door.

Looking back to the previous sequence, we find a further strengthening of the connection between Annie and Lydia and clarification of the significance of the birds (not an *explanation* of them). The bird that attacked Annie's door becomes associated with her isolation; earlier, while Lydia talked on the phone about her chickens' refusal to eat their feed, and Mitch and Melanie talked in the background, the only fragment of their conversation that was allowed to come through clearly was Melanie's question (indicating a painting) "Is that your father?" And as Melanie drove away, after her unsatisfactory, apparently

146

final conversation with Mitch, he gazed up at birds massing on the telegraph wires. The implication is not that the birds attack people with broken relationships—nothing so schematized; any temptation to interpret the film along these lines is quickly shattered by the more generalised attacks (on schoolchildren and townspeople) that make up much of the central section of the film. But a link of some kind between isolation and the threat the birds constitute has clearly been established.

The next sequence gives us the important dialogue between Mitch and Melanie and the first mass attack by the birds. The setting chosen for the dialogue—sand-dunes by the sea—and the action that introduces it—the couple clambering up the dunes in formal dress, Mitch carrying glasses and bottle—serve to emphasize the sense of precariousness in the relationship and in the very basis of the characters' lives: Melanie with her background of wild living and scandal, Mitch with his unsatisfactory home situation. With this precariousness of décor and situation intensified by our apprehension at the constant potential menace of bird attacks (the characters are out in the open again, unprotected) Melanie talks proudly of her job: she is studying semantics at Berkeley University and "helping a little Korean boy through school". Of Rome she says, "It was very easy to get lost there"; and so "I keep myself busy". It is the thinness of her life that one feels most—the sense that the "jobs" of which she speaks with pathetic complacency are feeble substitutes for any real sense of purpose or fulfilment; distractions more constructive than getting thrown into fountains in Rome, but distractions nonetheless. Then, with one of those swift transitions of which Hitchcock is such a master—the preceding frivolity of tone throwing into relief an intensity of feeling awkward and embarrassing in its abruptness—we pass from Melanie's aunt's myna bird to her relationship (or lack of it) with her mother. Gesture, stance and intonation, the setting of sea and dunes, the incongruity of the characters' physical position, are employed with a marvellous precision.

The effect of Melanie's revelations is to neutralise any lingering contempt we may feel for her triviality by showing us why she is like that—by making the triviality quite plainly a neurotic symptom over which she has little command; and to show us finally how superficial is her complacency, how easily shattered her confidence.

Their return to the children's party is watched by Lydia and Annie with similar expressions of anxiety, the developing relationship between Mitch and Melanie producing in both women the dread of aloneness and waste. Then, immediately, the bird attack begins.

The destruction of the children's party by the birds crystallises for us in a series of superbly realised images—the upsetting of cakes and cartons of fruit squash, and, particularly, the bursting of balloons—that awareness of fragility and insecurity that is the basis of the whole film. The scene ends with the tear-stained faces of two terrified children gazing anxiously up at the sky. That children are the victims of the attacks in these middle sequences is not mere sensationalism on Hitchcock's part. The children are completely innocent—there can be no 'reason' for the birds to attack them—and they are, even more than grown-ups, defenceless. The film derives its disturbing power from the absolute meaninglessness and unpredictability of the attacks, and only by having children as the victims can its underlying emotions of despair and terror be conveyed. To demand consistency and any form of divine or poetic justice from the attacks is to miss the point altogether.

The sequence depicting the attack of small birds down the chimney is the one point in the film where realisation —inevitably, one feels—falls short of conception. The superimpositions are very obvious here, and the 'attack' never looks like an attack—just a lot of frightened birds fluttering around. None of the characters involved receives even so much as a scratch (not surprising, as the vast majority of the birds are so obviously on separate strips of film). However, one sees why Hitchcock found the scene necessary. We have grown accustomed to the imposed and impeccable neatness and order of Lydia's house.

THE BIRDS: top, during the children's party; "only by
having children as the victims can its underlying emotions of despair and terror be conveyed"; and bottom,
Melanie and Mitch carry Cathy from the house where
Annie Hayworth has been pecked to death.

The heavy masculine décor shows us how she clings to the past, to the idea of her dead husband, and the determinedly imposed order suggests the importance the house and furniture have for her. Into this décor the birds irrupt: there is no safety from them, no shelter or screen behind which one can find security. When the attack is over, the ineffectual policeman questions the characters. Officials of the law are always ineffectual in Hitchcock: as representatives of a superficial, unnaturally imposed order they are unable, or refuse, to see the abysses: compare sheriff Al Chambers's dismissal of any suggestion of mystery in the Bates motel with the present policeman's inane refusal to accept the fact of the attack. While he talks to Mitch, Lydia stoops over the shattered crockery (smashed when Mitch upset the table to use it to barricade the fireplace), and, human beings forgotten, broods over her 'things', a look of bewilderment and desolation on her face. And we see Melanie watching the older woman, and are again aware of the resemblance between them. Melanie stares at her as if wondering: the scene is the clearest possible visual communication of the unspoken questions: "Has life any purpose? Has this woman's life any purpose? Has *my* life any purpose?" Melanie watches, while Lydia carefully, abstractedly straightens the portrait of her dead husband.

In a work of art as organic as *The Birds* it is possible to pick on almost anything as the 'key' to the meaning; but it is perhaps permissible to attach a particular importance to the sequence of Lydia's visit to Dan Fawcett's farm and the effect on her of what she sees there. First, the truck passing over that wonderfully evocative and disturbing landscape: calm-seeming, yet ominous in its stillness; beautiful, yet sombre beneath the dullish sky; the farm open to the sky amid its range of fields, the truck moving in long-shot along the dusty road. Then Lydia's entry into and exploration of the house ("Dan, are you there?"); her discovery of the cup-handles hanging uselessly from hooks on the kitchen dresser. The image, given strong impact by a sudden track-in that emphasizes the cup-handles by re-framing the shot and directly conveys to us Lydia's shock of perception, links back to the previous image of her bent over her own smashed tea-cups, thereby connecting Lydia with Fawcett. The corridor (everything ominously silent), the bedroom; more wreckage and disorder; the horrible-beautiful image of the dead sea gull caught in the smashed window; the empty double-bed; finally, in a series of relentlessly nearing shots, the mutilated body: we are given Lydia's experience directly, and we have sufficient knowledge of her now to appreciate its effect on her. The isolated man by the bed amid the wreckage of old, treasured furniture and bric-à-brac: Lydia's already precarious hold on life is cruelly undermined. We see her stagger, retching, speechless, back along the corridor, out past the bewildered farmhand; we see the truck travel rapidly back across the same still, ominous, beautiful landscape. From driver's seat position we see Mitch and Melanie together in the drive of the Brenner home as the truck sweeps up. They come to help the distraught woman as she clambers out, she looks at them, utters a terrible cry of despair, and pushes them violently aside.

The effect of the experience on Lydia calls to mind the effect on Mrs. Moore of her experience in the Marabar cave in E. M. Forster's *A Passage to India*. Hitchcock's image is more powerful and terrible than Forster's, it arises more naturally from its context and seems less 'applied': one is never quite convinced that an echo could mean all that. And film—as used by Hitchcock—can convey the experience to the spectator far more directly than can Forster to the reader. If *The Birds* lacks, certainly, the density and complexity of characterisation of Forster's novel, the comparison does not seem to me entirely disadvantageous to Hitchcock, for the Hitchcock of recent years is a more rigorous artist than Forster, quite free of those uncertainties of touch that Dr. Leavis has analysed in Forster's novels, and what may at first seem a comparative thinness in Hitchcock's films appears rather, on further reflection, as a toughness and self-discipline, a strict reduction of material to essentials to give extreme clarity and force to the presentation. In fact, a Hitchcock film—and *The Birds* is a particularly good example of this —is more analogous to a poem than a novel: Hitchcock focuses the attention and perceptions of the spectator, controls his reactions, through the rhythms of editing and camera-movement as a poet controls those of the reader through his verse-rhythms; and his films derive their value from the intensity of their images—an intensity created and controlled very largely by context, by the total organisation—rather than from the creation of 'rounded' characters.

Lydia's situation is defined more explicitly for us in her dialogue with Melanie as she sits in bed drinking tea: defined not only in the dialogue itself, but in gesture, expression and intonation. Before this, however, we have witnessed a new development in the relationship between Mitch and Melanie, a development touchingly conveyed in the tentative, tender kiss they exchange in the kitchen before Mitch goes to the Fawcett farm. Just the Hero kissing the Heroine, a weary Hollywood banality? Look again: as directed by Hitchcock, the moment conveys perfectly the beginning of sincerity in the characters, their acceptance of the human need for a relationship grounded in mutual respect and tenderness. It reveals the essentially positive bent of an undermining and ruthless film: in counterpoint to the breaking down of Lydia, the building up of a fertile relationship.

For it is precisely the dread of a solitary, sterile existence that terrifies Lydia. She is tormented not only by her immediate experience ("I keep seeing Dan's face") but by the loss of her husband, her sense of which the experience has abruptly intensified: "I wish I were a stronger person . . . I lost my husband four years ago . . . It's terrible how you depend on someone for strength". The emphasis is on the sense of valuelessness arising from a life lived without deep relationships. She has the tea-cup in her hand, a reminder, almost like a *leitmotiv,* of fragility and of her dependence since her husband's death on "things". She tells Melanie how she still gets up to get her husband's breakfast: "There's a good reason for getting out of bed . . . And then I remember . . ." She lives in a state of constant tension ("I wish I could relax—I wish I could sleep"). She feels her grasp on her children slipping, and again it is the loss of the father that is felt as responsible: "Frank . . . had the knack of entering into their world, becoming part of them. I wish I could be like that". Then suddenly: "Oh, I miss him!" It is a very basic reality that Hitchcock is presenting here. We are not to see Lydia as a neurotic woman: or, if neurotic, then made so recently by the frustration of certain basic human needs. Her fear of Melanie is not the outcome of an unhealthy involvement with her son, but of the dread of a life of loneliness and futility. The scene culminates in her cry, "But you see—I don't want to be left alone—I don't think I could bear to be left alone". It conveys positively a sense of the value of human relationships—marriage, family unity—and at the same time stresses their fragility: the fragility brought home to us and the characters by the birds. In the intimation we get of the close interdependence of the family and its resultant strength when the father was alive, we understand Mitch's individual strength. Yet the subtlety of the film, the delicacy of its feeling, lies in the way in which every point made is qualified by others, giving a touch of uncertainty to every action, every position, however simple it appears. We recall Mitch's conversation with Melanie on the dunes about their mothers. Melanie asked, "Do you know what a mother's love is?" and Mitch replied, "Yes, I think I do". His tone was so equivocal that she asked, "You mean it's worse?"; and his denial was hesitant, rather stiff, as if considering the possibility. Our sense of the value of relationships is qualified by the emphasis on the difficulties and complexities that they entail—the conflicting responsibilities that make it impossible that relationships be complete, that everyone be satisfied.

At the end of the scene in Lydia's bedroom, when

Melanie has agreed to go to the school to fetch Cathy, we are given again the positive trend, the reaching out towards the formation of viable relationships, in Lydia's tentative acceptance of Melanie as she thanks her for the tea and calls her for the first time by her Christian name: a very simple point, but, in its unobtrusive naturalness, a beautiful depiction of the beginnings of trust. There is a similar, more equivocal but no less beautiful instance in *Marnie,* where Marnie uses Mark Rutland's Christian name for the first time.

The next two attacks—on the fleeing schoolchildren and on the townspeople—scarcely require elucidation; but they furnish some of Hitchcock's most brilliant and disturbing images. On the one hand the world of order and tranquillity: the school, with its association of education, of the growing and developing young, of the transmission of tradition and culture, hence of mankind's hopes; the small, easy-going little town realised for us earlier in the film through its general store with its associations of community life, friendliness, familiarity, security. And on the other hand the birds, and their arbitrary destructiveness. The image of the terrified children running down the hill as the great flock of crows whirrs up from behind the school, looming over it and seeming to darken the sky; later images of disorder in the town, horses out of control pulling a cart that overturns, the unmanned firehose twisting and squirting uselessly; bring home to us in more general terms than before the frailty and precariousness of ordered, meaningful existence. One might single out particularly the stunning aerial long-shot of the town with its blazing centre, with bird after bird hurtling down to attack from behind the camera: *we* are suddenly the birds, looking down on defenceless humanity; but we are also human beings, and the image gives us a vertiginous sense of our own vulnerability.

Between the two attacks comes the debate in the café, with the two extreme attitudes to the birds expressed by Mrs. Bundy, the ornithologist, who refuses to believe the

154

attacks are happening and the town drunk, who airily proclaims, with considerable pleasure and satisfaction, that "It's the end of the world". Both attitudes are over-simplified and equally complacent; but "It's the end of the world" and "It's all impossible" are both attitudes likely to be common among the film's less perceptive spectators, and we know how carefully Hitchcock keeps his audience in mind when he prepares his films. By making these extreme attitudes explicit and ridiculous, Hitchcock prevents us from maintaining them during the crucial last stretches of the film. This is important to his purposes, despite the fact that the "end of the world" theory is logically tenable: we are nevertheless not to simplify the complex pattern of uncertainties the film presents into an ornithological *On the Beach*. By making us reject simple attitudes to the birds, Hitchcock focuses our attention on the development of character, situation and relationship, on the birds' *effect* rather than on the birds themselves, and on complex effects rather than simple effects.

It is after the second attack, back in the café, that we are placed (camera-wise) in Melanie's position in order to be told that we have caused the bird attacks and that we are evil. The accusation is made by the hysterical mother, and we respond promptly (through Melanie) by slapping her face. The incident is remarkable, and not nearly as simple as at first appears. Certainly, it is a direct attack on the audience, and we find it difficult to look in the face the woman who stares straight at us with such intensity. If Melanie is guilty, then certainly we are all guilty, for she is no more 'evil', and scarcely more com-placent, than we are; and there is peculiar appropriate-ness in the accusation coming from the one character in the film who is entirely without complacency—she ac-cepts the birds, terrified, as a terrible fact. Yet the accu-sation remains quite irrational and we are (Melanie is) right to reject it emphatically: Hitchcock is making us reject another over-simplified attitude: the birds have not been sent as a punishment for evil—they just *are*.

155

Yet there is another way in which we have provoked the attacks—as a cinema audience we have come demanding to be thrilled, perhaps shocked; demanding bloodshed and horror. We may recall Bruno Anthony remarking with severe distaste when the fairground attendant told him the public were flocking to see the murder-spot, "I don't think that's very nice". When, a few minutes before the accusation, we were given our birds' eye view, placed in the birds' position far above the town, we would certainly have been disappointed if the birds had flown away without doing anything, even as we shuddered at the helplessness of humanity. This is not the first time Hitchcock has made us aware of the impurity of our feelings: not the first time we have been encouraged to reveal our impure feelings in order to have them chastised.

This whole central section of attacks and debate opens the film out further: the birds are there for everybody, they exist for all of us. But the discovery of Annie Hayworth's dead body reminds us that they have a special significance for those who are alone. The sequence also brings home to us afresh our helplessness against the birds, in Mitch's furious, impotent gesture at them with a stone: the birds cannot be fought, no aggressive action can be taken against them. The force of this moment derives from the fact that Mitch is the 'hero' of the film, and (by the standards of Hitchcock's pre-*Marnie* heroes) unusually capable and stable, in control of most situations. The birds make the concept of 'hero' untenable.

There follows the boarding up of the house, and we reach the last phase of the film, where its underlying concerns and emotions are communicated with the greatest intensity. The house becomes a cage, as previously car and 'phone-box became cages: worse than a cage, a sunless box, in which the prisoners must come to terms with themselves and each other or finally succumb to the birds; and perhaps must die anyway.

If *The Birds* is about the Day of Judgement (another

THE BIRDS:
top, Mitch and
Melanie; and
bottom, "The
birds make the
concept of hero
untenable."

of Hitchcock's descriptions), then it is the value of life itself that is on trial. In this context, every gesture, every action, however trivial, becomes an object of closest scrutiny. Just after Cathy's questions and Mitch's admitted inability to answer them ("Why are they trying to kill people?"—"I wish I could say"), Lydia rises abruptly from the corner in which she is huddled. We watch her move into the foreground of the image, pick up a tray of cups and saucers, carry it out of the room, come back, resume her seat and her clenched, despairing attitude. Hitchcock shows us this in a single take in which nothing of any "importance" happens, and he shows us it deliberately and with emphasis, though it is an emphasis achieved quite naturally, entirely free from any pretentious ostentation; it can hardly be taken as a 'bit of business' to fill in while we wait for the next attack. It links Lydia to crockery again, of course, to the sense of fragility; but more than this, it typifies for us all those small routine actions that make up our day-to-day existence, and, by putting these in the context of the bird attacks, setting them against the tension shared by characters and spectators, raises in us the fundamental questions: Has life any purpose, any meaning? Is there any sense in our carrying on a daily routine with the knowledge that death may come to any of us at any moment, and must come, one day, to us all? Has anything a value that justifies this continuation? And these are not questions to which the film proposes any glib or comforting answers. The significance of Lydia's action itself is left ambiguous: is she rousing herself from her sense of futility for a moment to perform a positive action—however slight?— or is she merely mechanically repeating a meaningless and pointless routine? The ambiguity remains because of Hitchcock's refusal to resolve it through any kind of directorial comment, the motionless camera simply recording it objectively; it ushers in a whole series of similarly unresolved ambiguities in the last stages of the film.

In the moments before the attack on the house, Lydia is sunk hopelessly into her sense of futility—her cave-echo; it is Melanie who helps Cathy when the latter is sick, the mother seeming either unnoticing or indifferent. Then the attack begins, bringing the extraordinary shots of Melanie pressing herself back against the walls, against the sofa, upsetting the lamp-shade, as if seeking to hide herself from some unendurable scrutiny. But the girl's movements have themselves an ambiguity: they reveal an intolerable anguish, but in their abandonment one senses something almost sensual, like a voluptuous surrender. She is roused from this only by the necessity of bandaging Mitch's torn and bleeding hands.

The attack dies down, mysteriously and arbitrarily, at the very moment when it seems that no available barricades will keep the birds out. We have the three successive shots of ceiling and upper wall slowly filled by the characters' heads—Mitch, Melanie, Lydia, in that order—rising up from the bottom of the screen, hesitant and fearful, straining to catch sounds in the sudden silence. The shots are angled and framed so that the ceiling seems to press down on them, so that the very instant of relief seems laden with a sense of doom. There follows exhausted sleep, from which Melanie is aroused by the sound of birds restlessly fluttering somewhere in the house.

Why does she go upstairs alone? The question was put to me by one of Hitchcock's detractors: the implied answer was that there *is* no reason, it is merely a pretext for staging some cheaply sensational thrills. Let us answer it first on its own level: Melanie tries to rouse Mitch to get him to go, but he is sleeping exhaustedly, his hands sore and ripped and swathed in bandages, so she decides to go herself and let him sleep. She doesn't know that she is going to be trapped in a roomful of birds —she has heard noises which suggest that one or two birds may be getting in somewhere, and she goes to check: if there is any danger, she will come back and report to Mitch. This is a perfectly adequate, rational explanation supplied quite clearly by what we see on the screen; it accounts sufficiently for Melanie's conscious motivation, and indeed combines with her competent handling of Cathy to suggest the strength (albeit tentative) that her experiences are revealing in her character, in contrast to her self-prostration during the attack.

However, I would insist that the film as a whole invites us to ask the question on more serious levels, and I put forward the following suggestions: On a level just below the conscious, Melanie retains the sense, despite all she has been through, that nothing very awful will happen to *her:* she retains, that is, a residuum of complacency which has yet to be beaten out of her. This accounts for one aspect of the sequence—Hitchcock's use of subjective camera technique to enforce audience identification as Melanie climbs the stairs. This is similar in manner to Lila's exploration of the Bates menage, but not in effect: we dreaded Lila's entering the house, but we also wanted her to go in, to have our curiosity satisfied —we were still unsure what she would find. In *The Birds* we know what Melanie will find (she will find birds) and we are dragged up the stairs protestingly: we have already had so much bloodshed. We do, however, to some extent share her residual complacency: she is the heroine, a beautiful young girl, she will be rescued before anything very terrible happens to her: we must therefore share her disillusionment, her personal experience of the birds.

But the treatment of the attack itself reveals a deeper level of subconscious desire. Some of Melanie's gestures before the birds are gestures, again, of voluptuous surrender and prostration, her attempts to escape feeble. Her shallow sophistication and brittle smartness has been stripped away, revealing an apparent emptiness underneath; now she is giving herself to the birds as a terrible sort of fulfilment—almost like D. H. Lawrence's *Woman who rode away* accepting the sacrificial knife. And her frantic, yet curiously half-hearted and ineffectual, beating at the birds with her torch brings home to us again the inadequacy of our defences against all that the birds represent: the torch links with the car-hooter Melanie honked frantically, which clearly didn't frighten the birds

160

away (the attack just happened to end then); with the 'phone-box in which she was trapped, its possibilities of protection inadequate and of communication useless; with Mitch's powerful wooden barricades, which the birds easily peck through (impossible? Indeed it is; which only goes to prove that this isn't just a film about birds). Underlying the fight against the birds there is an inner conflict in Melanie between the tentative positive qualities that were emerging and a despairing desire for annihilation.

And I must insist that whether or not Hitchcock consciously intended these interpretations is quite immaterial: the only question worth discussing is whether they are sufficiently *there,* in the film, and I think they are. There is nothing arbitrary about this: the interpretations I have suggested become inevitable, it seems to me, if one sees *The Birds* in its context in Hitchcock's oeuvre, and there is no need to suppose them consciously worked out. If Hitchcock himself told me tomorrow that the whole sequence was shot purely to give the audience 'kicks', that the only reason why Melanie doesn't escape is that if she did the 'kicks' would stop, I would merely quote him my favourite aphorism of D. H. Lawrence: "Never trust the artist—trust the tale". The sequence, on which Hitchcock spent so much time and trouble, contains, in its closeup details of hands and face, gesture and expression, as the birds tear and batter the collapsing girl, some of the most horrific and beautiful images he has given us—some of the most desolate, conveying the extremity of human anguish. The appeal is not sadistic: there is too strong a sense of participation: we know it is *our* agony, *our* anguish that we are witnessing, for the birds are waiting for all of us.

But the most beautiful and moving moment of all is reserved for Melanie's regaining of consciousness downstairs. Mitch carries her down unconscious, Lydia rousing herself to help: the girl's suffering awakening in the woman her first positive reaction for some time, a sense of compassion. Mitch gives Melanie brandy. She comes round not knowing where she is, hands beating the air

161

to ward off imaginary birds. Mitch grips her hands, quiets them, their eyes meet, they exchange a long, deep look, and slowly she relaxes and subsides, her eyes still fixed on his, her face conveying a deep trust. The essential meaning of the film, it seems to me, is contained in that moment: that life is a matter of beating off the birds, and the only (partial) security is in the formation of deep relationships.

A bleak enough message; and in the last sequence of the film—the departure by car through the massed, waiting birds—the effect of bleakness is intensified by the uncertainties. For uncertainty is the keynote of the film: Hitchcock allows himself and us no easy comfort. Under this sense of judgment, of intense scrutiny, every action becomes ambiguous. The carrying of the love-birds out to the car: is it a touching gesture (through the child) of continuing faith, despite all, in the goodness of nature and the possibility of order, or an absurd clinging to a sentimental view of life, a refusal *still* to face reality? The mother's cradling of Melanie in her arms and the shot of their interlocking hands: is it a gesture of acceptance (hence creative and fertile) or a new manifestation of maternal possessiveness? Melanie's broken condition: does it represent the possibility of development into true womanhood, or a final relapse into infantile dependence? All these questions are left open: if we demand a resolution of them we have missed the whole tone and temper of the film. We can say, at best, that there is a suggestion of a new depth, a new fertility in the relationships—Lydia has become the mother Melanie never had. The point about the ending is that the degree of optimism or pessimism it is felt to contain must depend on ourselves: what Hitchcock gives us is the questions.

In all of Hitchcock's last five films the very last shot has great importance as the culmination of the whole action, the whole thematic progress. The ambiguity of the last shot of *The Birds* is dictated by these preceding uncertainties: the birds are letting them through; the birds

162

are massing for the next assault. This last shot represents a perfect balance of the sense of precariousness that runs through Hitchcock's work and the positive, therapeutic tendency that is an equally constant characteristic of it.

8. Marnie

THE GENERAL CRITICAL reception accorded to *Marnie* in Britain would appear quite staggeringly obtuse if one had not been well prepared for it by many precedents. However, as the notion that this film—one of Hitchcock's richest, most fully achieved and mature masterpieces—represents a falling-off, a proof of senility, or worse (he has become so cynical, apparently, about 'audience gullibility' that he just doesn't bother any more), it seems worth attempting to deal with the main lines of attack, removing certain false preconceptions as a preliminary to establishing what *Marnie* really is.

The following seem to be the main objections (in ascending order of intelligence):

1. The film is full of absurdly clumsy, lazy, crude devices, used with a blatant disregard for realism: hideous painted back-drop for Mrs. Edgar's street; ugly and obvious back-projection for Marnie's horse-riding (and, during the hunt, for Lil Mannering's); zoom-lens for the final attempted theft; red flashes suffusing the screen every time Marnie has a 'turn'; thunderstorms arriving coincidentally at climactic moments.

2. Connected with this technical naïveté, a psychological naïveté: Marnie's case is much too simple and schematized to be taken seriously, the single traumatic experience, as shown in the flash-back, wouldn't affect her in these ways. Besides, there are actual inconsistencies, obviously due to mere carelessness: Marnie passes a red chair during the Rutland office robbery and doesn't react; she almost touches a scarlet magazine, actually laying the pistol on it, when taking Mark's key, again without reacting.

163

3. (Though most people don't take the film seriously enough to reach this conclusion)—Marnie's 'case' is much too extreme for the film to have any universal validity.

The first objection, as usually phrased, seems to me based on that conventional rule-making that is invariably detrimental to art, since it seeks to impose limitations on the artist's freedom. There is absolutely no valid reason to forbid an artist the use of any method or device that suits his purposes; no valid reason why a film should be 'realistic', why a director shouldn't use obviously painted sets, back-projection, zoom-lens, etc., if the context justifies these things. The question is, then, not "should a serious director stoop to these?" but "Do they work?" Here we are clearly on more arguable ground; I can only state my case for believing that they do: the film would be weakened by their absence. Whether they were *consciously intended* to create certain effects I refuse—as usual—to discuss; though the very abundance and obtrusiveness of these devices makes it seem extraordinarily unlikely that Hitchcock merely "thought he could get away with it".

The back-drop of the ship needs to be considered as part of the set it dominates: the street in which Mrs. Edgar lives. Unbroken rows of tall ugly brick houses which give us a sense of imprisonment, claustrophobia, all possibility of freedom and openness shut out; at the end, the ship looming up ominously, as if blocking the exit. When we first see the image it is not precisely explicable, but it conveys admirably—if our responses are open, and free from preconceptions about 'realism'—the intolerable constriction of Marnie's life. Only at the end, when the crucial role played by a sailor in the arresting of her development becomes clear, does the huge, blocking ship take on a more precise symbolism. Perhaps something of the same effect—though it could scarcely have looked so ominous —could have been achieved with a real ship and a real street; but this would have sacrificed the most important aspect of all: the constrictedness of Marnie's life belongs essentially to the world of unreality, the trap she is caught

164

in is irrational and her prison will be finally shattered by true memory: at the end, the storm over, the sky a clear blue (as it never has been behind the ship before), she and Mark drive away past the ship, turning off where we had not previously been aware of the existence of a road. (They have arrived, by the way, apparently at nightfall, and leave ten minutes later in broad daylight: surprising that none of our literal-minded critical friends has commented on this, unless I have missed it). Far from being a fault, the false, painted set is a magnificent inspiration. I reject equally the notion that this and similar 'artificial' devices are 'ugly'. Ugliness or beauty in a film is a matter of context: we cannot look at a shot as if it were a painting, to be judged for its intrinsic aesthetic beauty. The street set, seen in context and understood, is very beautiful.

The first specimen of offending back-projection immediately precedes our first view of the offending ship. We see Marnie achieving her release from her adopted personality (slinky brunette) in the freedom of horse-riding. But, because of the back-projection, she doesn't look released at all, though her face tells us that she *thinks* she is. And of course that is the point. The back-projection gives a dream-like quality to the ride, but no sense of genuine release. The effect is clinched by the cutting: from the riding we cut immediately to the taxi driving up the mother's street toward the ship: change of 'vehicle' apart, it is presented as part of a single movement, a single state.

The use of zoom-lens and red suffusions brings us to something more fundamental in Hitchcock's art. Let it be insisted that they are not desperate attempts to cover up inadequacies in Tippi Hedren's performance: they are much too clearly in line with the whole audience-identification trend in Hitchcock's development to be explained away like that. The acting in *Marnie* is flawless: at no point does one feel that a player has failed to give Hitchcock precisely what is needed in any given shot. The blame —if blame there is—is Hitchcock's, not the admirable Miss Hedren's. The red suffusions are—obviously—more

165

than just blood symbolism. Because of her traumatic experience, the colour red, seen either under conditions of great tension or in a way that directly evokes the experience itself (the *spreading* red ink on the blouse sleeve, the red blotches on the jockey's shirt), acts as a release mechanism for Marnie's suppressed tensions—the tensions that are with her, to some extent, continually. Its immediate effect is to provoke a sort of hysterical swoon, a panic reaction, as the terrifying, buried memory forces itself dangerously near the surface of consciousness, which in turn produces a sense of unreality. Now, Hitchcock is not Preminger: he doesn't want merely to *show* us a woman caught in this condition, he wants to convey to us the feeling of the condition itself—wants us to experience it directly as Marnie experiences it, as far as that is possible. What better, simpler, more beautifully economical and direct way than by these red flashes that suffuse the whole screen, filling us, too, with a feeling of panic (we know no more than Marnie what they mean), conveying this sense of being plunged abruptly, arbitrarily, into unreality? Similarly with the zoom shots of the money. A director who wanted to *show* us Marnie at the moment when her compulsion to steal has been broken would use complex acting; Hitchcock wants us to *feel* her violent emotional condition, and the zoom shots, simple and crude as you please, offer much the most direct way of conveying this simultaneous attraction-repulsion.

As for the thunderstorm that accompanies and blends with the flashbacks, it is ridiculous to take it as coincidence, because the film doesn't work in the naturalistic manner to which such considerations are relevant. The stylized treatment of the storm (and the earlier one) forbids such an approach, as does the equally stylized use of the thunderclaps to punctuate the flashback and intensify certain of Marnie's shocks: the sailor's slamming of the door for example, cutting the child off from her mother, coincides with a thunderclap in the flashback and also, apparently, with one in present time; the thunderclaps emphasize what was most significant to the child

166

and what is most significant in memory. The use of storms to symbolize acute mental stress is so timehonoured (and has such respectable past employers) that it has surely become convention more than cliché.

But the final justification for these devices is not in these individual arguments, but in the way in which they are absorbed into their context, the context of the entire film. In his most recent work, Hitchcock has achieved such absolute mastery of his medium that he can feel free to use anything, to *dare* anything. This bold, direct use of devices one would normally shudder at is perfectly fitting in a film where every idea unerringly finds its most fluent, most economical, most direct expression, from the opening track on the yellow bag to the final long-shot of the car turning away as it passes the ship.

There are two possible answers to the accusation that a given film is psychologically naïve: that it isn't, and that it wouldn't matter if it were. In the case of *Marnie* the truth lies in a combination of these two. Scarcely more here than in *Psycho* is Hitchcock offering us the detailed analysis of a clinical case; the essentials of Marnie's mental disorder and of the preliminaries to its cure are given us with great force and clarity, but we are not given a *detailed* study of her behaviour, her symptoms or the minor components of her neurosis. To demand this is to demand an entirely different film: Hitchcock uses, as usual, all he needs and no more, and the film would be in no way improved if it went into Marnie's case in more detail. On the other hand, the psychology, though simplified, is by no means as simple as one would gather from reading the various dismissive accounts of the film. It seems to be the common assumption that one incident in childhood has caused Marnie's condition and the recollection of that incident automatically cures her. A moment's reflection will make it clear that the remembering is but one stage in the cure. We watch successive stages in it throughout the film, of which the honeymoon and attempted suicide, the breakdown after the 'free association' game, and the shooting of Forio are the most obvious; but the whole development of Marnie's relationship with Mark is movement towards cure. Nor are we given grounds for believing Marnie 'cured' at the end of the film: a start has been made, but the hopefulness of the last shots is offset by the reminder, through the mother, of the difficulty of outgrowing habitual attitudes.

And Marnie's troubles do not stem entirely from one traumatic experience. The child we see in the flashback is already a very disturbed child who can't bear a man to touch her, the mother already a hysterical, neurotic woman, a prostitute so filled with disgust at her work that she frantically beats with both hands the sailor who is trying to soothe and comfort her little girl. We needn't ask whether Marnie, at that age, has actually witnessed intercourse: she knows from her mother's attitude that something horrible and disgusting goes on behind that door whenever she is shut out; she is terrified of the sailor—who is gentle and kind—touching her; and it is clear, I think, that the image she somewhere retains of the twisted legs and her mother crying out in pain will stand subconsciously for her conception of sexual intercourse in her subsequent life. Further, because of the sailor's relationship to her mother, in killing him she is symbolically killing her father (just as in beating the man for touching Marnie, the mother is beating the man who deserted her when she became pregnant, refusing to allow the father any part in the child). Then there is Marnie's whole implied upbringing to be considered, at the hands of a mother who has indoctrinated her (if it were needed!) with a belief in the filthiness of sex and the evilness of men, and who has also withheld all love from her. The girl is possessed by the mother's attitudes, in danger of being swallowed up in her mother as Norman Bates was in his. Her entire life is a sort of symbolic prostitution, working for wealthy men, gaining their confidence—and interest—by the deliberate use of her charm (and by her very reticence and modesty: we remember Strutt's description of her "pulling her skirt down over her knees as if they were a national treasure", a gesture we watch her perform later at Rutland's), then taking their money and disappearing. Her involvement with her mother is summed up perhaps in her insistent mis-remembering of the childhood experience: "I hit him—I hit him with a *stick*". We have just seen her kill the sailor with an iron poker: it is the mother who, because of her 'accident', habitually carries a stick. The point gains further overtones from the fact that the mother has just attacked Mark Rutland, beating him with her hands as she beat the sailor: her attitude and Marnie's, her guilt and Marnie's, are interchangeable.

The money, of course, has a further significance: it is Marnie's way both of taking and of trying to buy love. The child who can't get affection steals; and Marnie uses what she steals to try to buy affection from her mother. Neither woman can give affection where it would be natural to give it: the mother's maternal impulses are instinctively suppressed and withheld from the daughter who is a constant reminder of her guilt (not merely of prostitution—the guilt has many ramifications); she lavishes affection on another child. And Marnie's substitute-object for her repressed sexual impulses is the horse Forio: "Oh, Forio, if you want to bite somebody, bite me!" The outline of a case history that Hitchcock gives us is perfectly satisfying psychologically: the more satisfying the more one follows the implications.

Hitchcock uses far more drastic simplifications, of course, to convey Marnie's symptoms. If he were offering a clinical study, they would be unpardonable. But he is offering—to anyone reasonably responsive—much more than that, and the simplifications (those red suffusions again: Marnie's reactions to red, to the thunderstorms, to tapping, her recurring nightmares) constitute an artistically valid shorthand. Again, what seem to many faults are, properly regarded, shining virtues. With superb daring, Hitchcock sweeps aside all the distracting encumbrances of detailed psychological analysis—distracting that is, from the real theme of the film. It is by stylising in this way that Hitchcock prevents the significance of his film from being limited to Marnie's 'case.'

169

As for the inconsistencies—the moments when Marnie *doesn't* respond to red—the two instances are quite distinct and must be considered separately. The instance of the chair in the office which we see Marnie pass twice during her robbing of the safe one would be inclined to pass over with a shrug—the objection is the merest naturalistic pedantry—did it not offer a very interesting example of how a great artist operates and raise a fundamental question. We shall not appreciate any work of art if we remain insensitive to the kind of realisation it offers at any given point—if, instead of maintaining an open, sensitive, flexible response we set ourselves to deliberately working *against* it. In *Marnie* it is inherent in the 'red' shorthand that it can be used, quite arbitrarily, as Hitchcock pleases, precisely because it is not a naturalistic device, as long as the film evokes the required response in the spectator; since the red chair is never connected visually with Marnie, we do not, if we are working *with* the film, respond to it as we do to the gladioli or the jockey's shirt. It is like the famous question of "How many children had Lady Macbeth?" At one point she has "given suck", at another Macbeth "has no children". Now, there are all kinds of possible explanations if we care to think of them: Lady Macbeth's child had died, Macbeth was her second husband, she was a parvenue ex-wet-nurse, etc. Similarly, explanations can be found in *Marnie* for the heroine's indifference to the offending chair (not the least convincing being that she has presumably seen it every day for some weeks and had plenty of chance to get used to it). But such explanations are irrelevant: neither play nor film operates in that way, and if we ask such questions we are simply failing to respond to the kind of realisation that is being offered. Both Macbeth's childlessness and his wife's breast-feeding have clear dramatic relevance in their contexts; similarly, important use is made of that chair, but it is a use different from the use of other red objects elsewhere. One could quote in this connection Hitchcock's delightful response when asked why James Mason's supposed wife in *North by Northwest* comes in to ask her husband to receive guests who don't seem to exist: "I know nothing about it. I don't know the lady in question, I've never met her. I don't know why she came in then, or why she said that . . ."

Hitchcock uses the burglary sequence to convey to us, by the now familiar means of direct experience, the constant tension under which Marnie lives and the precariousness of her whole existence, which can hang on something as slight as a dropped shoe. We see her prepare to burgle the safe, leave the office door open, work the combination. Then the camera is set down for a long take in which we see her, in long-shot, in the centre of the screen, carry out the theft. On the right of the screen is the red chair, on the left an empty passageway. Then a cleaner appears round the corner at the end of the passageway, and begins to mop, drawing nearer and nearer as Marnie, quite unaware of her, goes on lifting the money. The tension depends on several factors. We share Marnie's own tension, certainly—we become aware of the tight-rope precariousness that is her whole life. But our tension is greater than hers: we know the charwoman is there, she doesn't. Further, we want her to get away with it, and we are slightly ashamed of wanting this: stealing is wrong; more than that, stealing isn't going to help Marnie, who clearly needs psychological aid—getting away with it won't help her. It is scarcely too much to say that this tension between our emotional involvement in Marnie's wishes and our rational awareness that their fulfilment would do her nothing but harm is the basic suspense-principle of the film. The tension is assisted by a characteristically daring use of sound (or lack of it). The sound track here is doubly subjective: we don't hear the slap of the cleaner's mop because Marnie, from inside the inner office, can't hear it; we hear only the slightest muffled sound, scarcely audible, of the heavy safe door closing, because that is all the cleaner (who, as we find out later, is very deaf) would hear. And counter-pointed with all this, and intensifying it, is a colour tension. The cleaner, far left, is dressed in a cerise smock; the scarlet chair occupies an almost exactly symmetrical position on the right of the screen, producing a jarring clash that acts on the eye as the other tensions on mind and ear.

And the red magazine? That is a very different matter. Marnie looks straight at it, lays the pistol on it; and her not reacting to it *at that moment in the action* is precisely the point. She has just shot Forio after the accident: an action of highly complex significance. Firstly, there is the purely physical shock experience, the importance of which Hitchcock's realisation of the accident emphasizes: seldom, surely, has physical sensation been so intensely conveyed in a film. There is the use of subjective time: the repeated tracks towards the wall, giving us a time monstrously prolonged, convey that agonising nightmare-feeling of an interminable moment we get at times of extreme terror; then the camera positions and the rhythm of the cutting are conceived so as to convey the maximum physical impact. We remember Marnie's fear of death— her immediate association of the idea of death with herself—in that peculiarly revealing moment in the 'free association' game; and here she, and the spectator, are brought face to face with the possibility of death in an unusually violent and, for Marnie, particularly appropriate form: a helpless, uncontrollable whirling towards destruction. But it is Forio who dies, Marnie who insists (from any rational point of view unnecessarily) on killing him herself. The shooting is, clearly (though we don't know it at the time), a re-enactment of the killing of the sailor, a reliving without remembering of the traumatic experience: the death of the horse is linked with the end of the memory later by Marnie's "There—there now". And there is another point: the love Marnie lavishes on Forio has been a substitute for sexual fulfilment; the shooting of the horse occurs very shortly after the first obviously hopeful signs of her being capable of achieving a valid relationship with a man. Coming straight from the shooting, in a trance-like state of shock, Marnie no longer responds to red. Her tensions are partially resolved; she has reached a stage beyond that where they require a simple stimulus to secure their release in panic-reactions. It is immediately afterwards, it will be remembered, that Marnie finds herself unable to steal: the obsessive-compulsive behaviour is breaking down, because the tensions that necessitated it are disintegrating. She is ready for the final stage in the preliminaries to cure: the domination of the past through memory.

Before I leave the red suffusions, there is one more point to note about them, which is that they are used not only as a convenient shorthand, but structurally. They are not random, but form a clear progress. Each one takes us a step nearer the reality of the traumatic experience, and Marnie a step deeper in her descent into memory. First, her reaction to the red gladioli associate her tensions—consequently her compulsive behaviour—with her mother; and with her mother's relationship with the child Jessie. The second red suffusion occurs during the first dream, in the mother's house, bringing together a number of other associations: the tapping (associated at the end of the scene with the mother's stick, hence with the 'accident'), the sensation of cold, etc. The fourth suffusion associates Marnie's tensions with thunderstorms (in Mark's office), the remaining component of the memory. The most obvious progression is formed by the third, fifth and sixth suffusions: the spreading red ink on the white sleeve, the scarlet blotches on the jockey's shirt, the scarlet hunting-jacket (given a disturbing glare by the lighting), which lead naturally to the presentation of the memory itself, stylised and subjective, of the bloodstained sailor's shirt.

As for that third objection (that Marnie's 'case' is too extreme to have universal validity), I seem to have invented it myself, since I cannot recall encountering it anywhere, but it seems worth answering. I have already suggested a partial answer: we are not concerned with Marnie's case simply as a case. Hitchcock gives us here, in fact, a sort of quintessence of neuroticism rather than a clinical case history, and if Marnie is extreme, she represents an extreme of something relevant to us all: the grip of the past on the present. If few of us are Marnies, there

173

is something of Marnie in all of us. We are all to some extent dominated by the past, our present psychological liberty limited and interfered with by unremembered and unassimilated past experiences. Even Mark Rutland, who, as created in the film, is as exceptionally free of the past as Marnie is exceptionally gripped by it, is led to recognize motivations behind his behaviour of which he was not entirely aware. Nonetheless, this balancing of one extreme by another is one way in which Hitchcock universalises his theme, and one must not allow oneself to be prevented, by the fact that the film is so firmly and deliberately centred on the evolution of Marnie herself, from giving due attention to the character of Mark and the positive values he embodies. Indeed he represents a new stage in the development of Hitchcock's heroes: not only is he unusually free of inner compulsions and of his own past life, he sees clearly and accepts the fact of the inextricability of good and evil—the fact that every moral action carries within it its inextricably interwoven thread of immorality—that we have seen as one of the essential components of Hitchcock's moral sense.

Another way in which *Marnie* achieves universal significance is through the reminder—hardly necessary if we are familiar with Hitchcock's past work, but clearly if simply realised in the film and necessary to its completeness—that anyone, given the circumstances, could be Marnie. Consider the ending: Marnie, the traumatic experience remembered, comes out of her mother's house with Mark. The storm is over, it is broad daylight. A gang of children is playing beside the step. They interrupt their game to look at the haggard woman in the riding suit: shot of them gazing up at Marnie, of Marnie returning their gaze. We remember the Marnie of the flashback, a child of about this age, caught in an experience she had done nothing to bring about (the fact that her panic precipitates the killing can hardly be held to her blame) and over which—and its consequences for herself—she could exercise no control. As Marnie and Mark drive away, the children resume their play, a ritualistic game with a chant

174

we heard when we saw Marnie first arrive at the house: "Mother, mother, I am ill./Send for the doctor over the hill . . ."

Retrospectively, we can see the point also made through Jessie, the little girl Mrs. Edgar looks after, and on whom she lavishes the affection she cannot give Marnie. The use of Jessie is quite complex. She seems at first merely to be there to provoke Marnie's jealousy: a jealousy childish, certainly, but rendered with extreme poignance. One instance, moving in itself, but more moving in the context of the whole, since it is one of the unifying links used to establish the film's essential progression: Marnie has just given her mother the fur wrap, draping it tenderly round her neck. Mrs. Edgar calls Jessie to have her hair brushed, and removes the wrap, laying it aside. Marnie kneels beside her mother, placing her own head in the position necessary for her hair to be brushed. Mrs. Edgar moves her away, saying, "Marnie, mind my leg". Jessie, with a triumphant glance at Marnie, sits on the edge of the chair, pressed right up against the aching leg, and turns to Mrs. Edgar, who begins to brush her hair, which is roughly the same colour and length as Marnie's. Close-up of Marnie watching with sad eyes, then subjective shot from her viewpoint. The camera tracks in on the hair and the brush, which moves over it with such tenderness. It is a beautiful example of Hitchcock's ability to make the spectator share, hence understand, a character's feelings. At the end of the film, after her recalling of the past, Marnie kneels again in the same position beside her mother's chair. Close-up of Mrs. Edgar's hand reaching out to touch her daughter's hair. Then, instead, she moves restlessly: "Marnie, you're achin' my leg". Marnie gets up, resigned. Mark Rutland takes her, and strokes and tidies and smoothes her hair with his hands, saying, "There, that's better," and Marnie accepts the action. The moment—so unobtrusive and unforced—is perhaps (more even than the flashback) the climax of the film: it expresses, with that simplicity which is the prerogative of genius at the

175

height of its powers, the transference towards which the whole film has been progressing.

But Jessie is also used to parallel Marnie. We see her first through Marnie's eyes, and therefore share Marnie's reaction to her; but Marnie's treatment of her is too unkind, too neurotic, and we soon dissociate ourselves from it and see the child as essentially vulnerable and pathetic, fatherless, left all day by her mother, quite at the mercy of an obviously neurotic old woman who pampers her extravagantly and (no doubt) fills her head with nonsense about the bestiality of men, and a neurotic young woman who is irrationally beastly to her. The child's likeness to Marnie both in situation and appearance (Mrs. Edgar is reminded of Marnie's hair when she was little) is emphasized, and we see the vulnerable child and the woman who has never been able to grow up as interchangeable: Jessie could be Marnie—any of us could be Marnie.

The theme of *Marnie* is universalised partly through Lil, Mark's sister-in-law. She is presented throughout as a contrast to Marnie, in personality and general orientation as much as in appearance. Hitchcock gives us through her a marvellous and touching picture of female sexuality —she *exudes* it in all her scenes with Mark—to set against (and set off) Marnie's frigidity. Yet her behaviour is in some ways curiously like Marnie's: her lying (about her wrist), eavesdropping, prying into others' private papers, underhand destructiveness (inviting Strutt to the party), parallel Marnie's criminal activities. We saw in *Psycho* how the compulsive behaviour of a psychotic was made relevant to us all by its parallel in the compulsive behaviour of a 'normal' person; similarly in *Marnie*, the 'normal' Lil acts in a way that borders on the compulsive, providing an extension into normality of Marnie's neuroticism.

A final means whereby Hitchcock universalises *Marnie's* significance: almost exactly halfway through the film, during the honeymoon cruise, Mark tells Marnie about a beautiful jungle flower. When you get close to it, you find that its intricate pattern is composed of thousands of

176

tiny insects, who have adopted this formation as protective camouflage against birds. The immediate application of this to Marnie herself is obvious enough: she can only survive by preserving a carefully cultivated, artificial exterior personality; this shattered, she would be in danger of disintegrating into fragments and of becoming a prey to 'the birds'. But by expressing it in this parabolic form at this central point in the film where Marnie's 'artificial' personality is endangered by the relationship forced on her by Mark, Hitchcock gives the idea far wider extension: the whole *Vertigo-Psycho* theme of the relationship between appearance and reality is suddenly crystallised in a single image, an image that epitomizes the basic Hitchcock assumption (leading theme of *The Birds* itself) of the precariousness of order, the glimpse of the underlying chaos when that order is disturbed.

In *Marnie,* in fact, most of the concerns underlying Hitchcock's recent films become fused. Most obvious are the links with *Psycho*. There is the mother/child relationship, bringing with it the theme of the swallowing up of one personality by another: Marnie is in danger of becoming her mother—in all essentials—as Norman became Mrs. Bates. In both cases this involvement arises from a mutual guilt, which in *Marnie* becomes an especially complex entanglement, both mother and child sharing in the killing, each provoking the other's reactions. Marnie herself is a curable Norman Bates; or a combination of Norman and Marion Crane. With this comes the characteristic Hitchcockian preoccupation with the contrast between seeming and being, the public mask and the private truth, appearance and reality. The film contains a number of striking (whether intentional or not) reminiscences of *Psycho:* Marnie's mother lurching downstairs with her stick immediately evokes—in stance, attitude, rigidity of movement—Mrs. Bates; Mrs. Edgar's attitude to men is Mrs. Bates's attitude to girls; her attack on Mark, beating him with raised fists, reminds us of Mrs. Bates's knife attacks; at the end of the film, when Marnie and Mark leave, lighting and make-up give Mrs. Edgar's face a corpse-like appearance—she seems almost an embalmed body, a living death.

But there is a less obvious link to a previous film, that can be put like this: had Hitchcock elected to tell *Marnie* from the point of view of Mark Rutland, we would have something strikingly resembling (if significantly different from) *Vertigo.* Look at the film from this point of view and the triangle Mark-Marnie-Lil closely resembles in essentials the triangle Scottie-Madeleine-Midge. Marnie first intrigues, then fascinates Mark because of her inscrutability and mysteriousness, her very abnormality. Scottie falls in love with Madeleine because she is remote, dream-like, inaccessible; and in one of the crucial sequences of *Marnie,* Marnie rounds on Mark with "Talk about dreamworlds! You've got a pathological fix on a woman who's not only a criminal but who screams if you come near her". Like Scottie, Mark rejects a known reality for this "dream-world". Lil's ineffectual struggle to win him back reminds us of Midge's parody-portrait. And as in *Vertigo* our reactions are complicated by a certain sympathy for the rejected woman. Lil is at once more ruthless and less mature than Midge; yet the moment when she watches Marnie and Mark drive away after the wedding has something of the force of Midge's final exit down the corridor: a subjective shot puts us, for a matter of seconds, in Lil's place, we watch the car disappearing down the drive. Then the camera rests unbrokenly on her face as Uncle Bob goes on and on with his grumbling about Mark's recklessness with money, and we see that the car was bearing Lil's life away with it.

But such parallels cannot be pressed too far: ultimately, it is the differences behind the resemblances that are important. If Mark is Scottie, then he is Scottie without the vertigo: a Scottie become mature, responsible and aware. Perhaps the most striking thing about *Marnie* is this new development in the Hitchcock hero, for of all Hitchcock's male protagonists, Mark is the one most in charge of situations, most completely master of himself and his environment, most decisive and active and purposive. In a sense, he is the reverse of Scottie: where Scottie struggled to re-create the dream of Madeleine—the illusory Idea—Mark struggles to destroy the unreal shell of Marnie—the protective exterior—in order to release the real woman imprisoned within it.

His capability is insisted on as specifically a freedom from the trammels of the past, embodied particularly in his attitude to Stella, his dead wife. When the branch shatters the display cabinet in his office and Marnie solicitously picks up a damaged vase from Stella's pre-Columbian collection, he takes it from her and casually smashes it, saying, "Well, we've all got to go sometime". In this attitude to the ancient vase he is rejecting more than domination by the memory of his dead wife: he is symbolically rejecting the whole grip of past on present. And later, at the party, he has no hesitation in allowing people to think he knew Marnie—suspiciously—for several years before their marriage. Lil, startled, begins, "Before Stell . . .?" and Mark cuts in with an off-hand, "Yes, didn't you know?" Lil's suspicions worry Marnie: "Lil thought . . ."; but Mark merely remarks, "I don't give one infinitesimal dime what Lil thought or thinks". It is this freedom from the past (combined with this refusal to be limited by 'what people think') that makes him peculiarly able to help Marnie. The character carries, in the context of the film and of Hitchcock's work as a whole, great moral force. He embodies a powerful and mature life-quality that is set against Marnie's helpless readiness to let the past swallow her: that corpse-like face of the mother represents the spiritual death from which Marnie has been saved.

Given this vitality, it is fitting that Mark should also embody a clear-eyed acceptance of the inseparability of good and evil in such a complex world. In answer to Marnie's "Talk about dream-worlds . . .", he is able to reply, with a calm accepting smile, "Well, I didn't say I was perfect". It is partly this acceptance of necessary moral imperfection that gives him his maturity—seen as a willingness to accept responsibilities and follow them

179

through whatever this entails. The morality of the film is, in an unobtrusive way, very unconventional and subversive, arising from the assumption that a 'pure' morality is impotent and useless, that often the only true morality is *conventionally* immoral. Hence Mark *forces* Marnie to marry him, using quite unfair and unscrupulous means: it is the only way he can help her. Not that he is acting altruistically, merely for her good: he is quite clear on the boat in referring to himself as a "sexual blackmailer"— *"Some other* sexual blackmailer would have got his hands on you". Equally clear, however, is his distinction between himself and other potential "blackmailers": his description makes us think of the lecherous but conventionally moral —indeed, self-righteous—Strutt, and an essential difference is that Mark is aware of and accepts the impurity of his motivation.

The complexity of the values embodied in Mark—of our attitude to him—seems hardly to have been noticed, but its reality is perhaps attested by the directly contradictory reactions the character provokes. Different people have said to me that Mark is (a) incredible because such a saint and (b) unacceptable because morally so vicious. Since he embodies—so actively and energetically—the underlying moral assumptions of the later Hitchcock, it is worth considering his position in some detail.

When he forces Marnie to marry him he is acting neither simply for her nor simply for himself. If he let her go he would be (as he tells her in the café) "criminally and morally responsible" for her actions and for what became of her. If she were caught she would go to prison: we must remember that he has not yet fathomed the depth of her psychological disturbance: if she has not exactly responded to his kisses, she has managed not to recoil from them. But it is equally clear that he forces her into marriage because he loves her and wants her. He is motivated, in other words, not so much by a desire that she be helped, as by a desire that *he* should help her: he wants her cure to develop out of their relationship. And his desire for her, it is clear, is aroused partly by the very

180

fact that she needs help: his love for her is not entirely distinct from desire to possess, control, even—Pygmalion- or Scottie-like—create. It is his intellectual interests, zoology and psychology, instinctual behaviour, that first attract him to Marnie: she is both an interesting 'case' and a potentially dangerous animal. This latter comparison is developed visually as well as in the dialogue (for example during Mark's disclosure in the car that he loves her: "You think I'm some kind of animal you've trapped" —"That's right, you are"): as they are about to leave the roadside café Mark watches her as he would watch a dangerous animal; on the boat, Marnie cowers from him against the sofa arm, and we are irresistibly reminded of a dangerous yet terrified animal cowering from its tamer; later, when she "gets herself up like a cat-burglar", the camera restlessly follows her movements as she paces the bedroom like a caged animal, conveying her sense of constriction and her nervous restlessness to the audience. With all her repressions, she represents something more vital, potentially more alive, than the Rutland environment.

Marnie makes Mark realise the nature of his attraction to her in the car when he makes his 'proposal'. Obeying the dictates of 'acceptable' morality would make him powerless to help her. It is only by following through his basic instinctive drives that anything can be achieved, and those drives, necessarily impure in themselves, demand morally impure methods of fulfilment. The implied 'doctrine' (if it can be called that) is of course very dangerous, and the dangers are not minimized by the film: the emphasis given to the attempted suicide and Mark's panic-stricken searching of the ship is but the most obvious example.

The attempted suicide is provoked by Mark when, faced with Marnie's dread of sex, he promises not to sleep with her and then a few nights later breaks that promise. There is no more devastatingly beautiful scene in the whole of Hitchcock, and the beauty arises not merely from the fluency of expression but from the awareness of moral complexity that underlies it. Mark, who has been drinking

181

heavily (to weaken the grip of his superego?), desperate from frustrated desire—which is both desire *for* Marnie and desire to help her—follows her into the bedroom. She asks him to leave if he doesn't want to go to bed; he replies that he "very much wants to go to bed". She understands, cries out "No!" in panic, and he rips off her nightdress. The sequence of shots is then as follows: 1. Marnie's bare feet and legs. 2. Her head and bare shoulders. Marks says, "Sorry, Marnie". 3. Both of them. He removes his dressing-gown, wraps it round her. She stands stiffly, in a sort of tense, rigid resignation. He kisses her. 4. Overhead shot of the kiss. His hands stroke her tenderly. 5. Low-angle shot. We see his lips moving over her unmoving, expressionless face, her lips making no response whatever. She is like a statue. His protective gestures—the dressing-gown, his stroking hands, his tenderness—tenderness inseparable from sexual passion— combines with her hopeless, unresponsive immobility to give us that sense of a longing for the unattainable that is the essence of *Vertigo;* the angles—overhead shot to suggest protectiveness and solicitude, low-angle to reveal in detail the tenderness of the man's touch—add to the desolating sense of his helplessness, his inability to reach her. 6. Close-up, Marnie's face. She sinks down, the camera following her, peering into her eyes with their terrible, unfathomable emptiness, like the eyes at the beginning of *Vertigo*. 7. Close-up, Mark's face, huge and ominous, shadowed, the eyes seeming to bore into her. We share simultaneously his pity and desire and her terror, we see how in him desire for her and desire for power *over* her are not clearly distinguished. 8. Close-up, Marnie again. Then the camera pans round across the bedroom, coming to rest on a port-hole. A sexual symbol, certainly, which conveys the sexual act; but more than that: for beyond the port-hole is the sea, empty, desolate, grey, and the shot also completes our emotional response to the whole scene. The complexity here is both moral and emotional, conveying to the spectator a sense at once of the beauty and the tragic pathos of human relationships.

MARNIE: top left, Marnie (Tippi Hedren) discarding an identity; top right, Marnie and Mark (Sean Connery)—the stable; and left, the honeymoon.

The scene offers one of the purest treatments of sexual intercourse the cinema has given us: pure in its feeling for sexual tenderness. Yet what we see is virtually a rape. To the man it is an expression of tenderness, solicitude, responsibility; to the woman, an experience so desolating that after it she attempts suicide. Our response depends on our being made to share the responses of both characters at once.

Mark's treatment of Strutt constitutes one of the clearest moral statements in Hitchcock. In an impure world, he has no hesitation in resorting to the most impure means—blackmail—to defeat the conventionally pure Strutt. He is quite clear about this—and Hitchcock makes it quite clear where, as between Mark and Strutt, the moral superiority lies. What gives Mark this right? Simply that he is acting for life, against the deadening self-righteousness of conventional morality; his right derives from the rightness of his instinct, which is basically sexual instinct. For if evil in Hitchcock's late work (Psycho) derives primarily from perverted sexuality, so good has its roots in true sexuality and the true flow of sympathy that stems from it. Only the essential validity of Mark's feeling for Marnie—feeling not altruistic, not 'pure', because not distinct from power-urge, but rooted in his sexuality—justifies his actions. If Psycho was a mainly negative statement, its magnificent fearlessness and robustness implied a strong underlying positive; and that positive finds its expression, quite unequivocally, in Marnie. Mrs. Edgar, when she attacks Mark, may remind us of Mrs. Bates with her knife, but Mrs. Bates was irresistible, whereas Mrs. Edgar is easily overpowered by a man who embodies qualities which have no equivalent in Psycho.

It is Mark's self-awareness, and his acceptance of necessary moral impurity, that makes him able to deal with the business world effectively (he has put the firm of Rutland back on its feet). That business world is superbly rendered in the film, through four clearly differentiated and evaluated characters: Mr. Strutt, Mr. Ward, the man who approaches Marnie at the race-track, and

184

Uncle Bob. Ward's absent-mindedness is more than a necessary plot-manoeuvre, and a little more than a manifestation of that balanced, ironic Hitchcockian humour that has its contribution to make to the overall tone of *Marnie;* it suggests the inorganic nature of the man's life, the failure of 'business' to engage the human being caught up in its machinery. The man at the race-track, with his air of furtive indecency and his inability to meet Mark's eyes, suggests a whole sordid world of petty intrigue financial and sexual. And if the business world is presented slightly more sympathetically in Uncle Bob—who is after all a Rutland, with something of the more humane culture the Rutlands represent—his financial preoccupation, expressing itself in a rigidity of stance, a hardening of the mouth, is morally placed by its juxtaposition with Lil's emotional preoccupation, her sense of loss as Mark and Marnie drive away.

But the Rutland culture itself is by no means endorsed by the film. Mark's father, and the environment in which we see him—his home, his furniture, his estate, his stables —represents a true gentility, a mellowness, that shows up the world of the Strutts for the raw inhuman thing it is; yet Hitchcock emphasizes the hermetic aspect of this world, and its air of stagnation, and eventually, in the fox-hunt, the unthinking brutality with which it can associate itself (the hunters, beautiful in long-shot, made to look stupid and trivial by the suddenly cut-in back-projection shot of Lil bouncing complacently up and down on horseback). The sense of abrupt alienation Marnie feels on seeing and hearing the insensitive laughter of the hunters as they watch the fox torn to pieces is marvellously communicated to the audience: communicated, as usual in this film, with such economy and directness: this is not mere anti-fox-hunting propaganda, but a sudden revelation of the limitations of what has hitherto seemed a generally attractive world, limitations of sensibility that go with the sense of stagnation. The point—the necessary linking up of our diverse responses—is made through Marnie's denunciation of Lil after the accident: "Are you

185

still in the mood for killing?" The reference is plainly to much more than the death of the fox: one thinks at once of Lil's compulsive destructiveness in inviting Strutt to the party. Again, the comparison of Marnie at several points in the film to a wild animal makes us connect her at once with the fox, and the callousness of the hunters links with Strutt's self-righteous vindictiveness: his word "victimized" draws together a number of emotional threads. The Rutland world is without real vitality or flexibility, the father's responses limited and obvious. His remarks on travelling (when Mark and Marnie return from their honeymoon) sum up the enclosedness of his existence. The way of life the Rutland home represents is 'placed' by Mark himself: by his flexibility of response, his alertness, his decisiveness and vitality, his range of interests.

But, crucially important though Mark is, both in relation to this film and to Hitchcock's whole development, it is Marnie's film, and in her Hitchcock gives us the most definitive statement so far of that 'therapy' theme we have seen running through all his work. Every sequence of *Marnie* is constructed as a necessary stage in the breaking down of Marnie's defensive barriers, of all that prevents her being fully alive. Hitchcock emphasizes her rootlessness. Consider the opening of the film: we are shown first a yellow bag, which the camera follows in a tracking-shot. The camera slows down, and the bag is given a context: a woman with long, black-dyed hair in a grey suit and high heels, walking stiffly and in a straight line. Then the camera stops altogether, and she in turn is given a context: a deserted station platform, empty trains, silence, no life anywhere. It is in this way that we see Marnie for the first time, and the image is immediately disturbingly evocative. The colour assists this effect strongly: the yellow bag looks strikingly incongruous, adding to our sense of instability; apart from it, everything—platform, trains, station roofs, gasometer —is grey or grey-blue, steely and cold. Marnie is continually shown against or associated with these colours throughout the film: they are the colours of her mother's house, where all the rooms have grey or blue-grey wall-papers; of the ship at the end of the mother's street; of the office interiors that epitomize the business world; of the washroom and the cell-like lavatory in which she waits before the theft; of other stations; of the exteriors of the ship on which Mark and Marnie spend their honeymoon; of stormy skies, and of the sea itself, whose desolation contrasts so movingly with the enclosed, flower-laden luxury of the cabin, the reality and the pretence of Marnie's life. The incongruous yellow becomes important later in the film, where it is frequently associated with the Rutland home: Mark's father's yellow waistcoat, his yellow cake (a foolish, trivial example? Look at the visual emphasis it gets, at its placing in the composition), the yellow chrysanthemums in the hall, yellow roses in Marnie's room, yellow-gold lampshades, etc. In that crucial scene where Mark sleeps with (or rapes?) Marnie, he wears yellow pajamas and yellow dressing-gown—the dressing-gown in which he encloses her as he lowers her to the bed (their cabin has yellow and greyish décor). Marnie herself wears yellow (but a pallid yellow) in the scene where Mark brings Forio to her, the moment that brings her for the first time close to him (look at their exchanged glances) if only in gratitude. In the Rutland house the yellow is always the focal point of the composition, in which the colour-range suggests natural surroundings, with a hint of the autumnal: browns, dark greens, occasional dull reds.

Marnie is continually travelling, by train, car, taxi, ship, on horseback, moving from one place to another but getting nowhere—a point that the dream-like quality given by the back-projection to the horse-riding sequence epitomizes. The Rutland world, on the other hand, is static, even stagnant: old Mr. Rutland never travels, it is "a nasty business". The two extremes throw into relief the movements of Mark, every one of which has a purpose and precipitates a new development; whereas Marnie's true progress is only incidentally related to her movements from place to place.

Though identification-patterns in *Marnie* are more com- plex than in *Psycho* or the first half of *Vertigo,* it is broadly true that we are made to share Marnie's tensions through- out the film. Suspense is used always to convey the con- stant strain under which she lives, so that the extreme points of her tension are the extreme points of ours. We share, too, then, her first moment of genuine relaxation, when Mark brings her Forio; above all, we share her sense of release, at the image of the blood-soaked shirt that fills the whole screen, fulfilling and hence exorcising the intimations of unknown horror given by the red suf- fusions. But our suspense is not the simple thing it may at first appear: our tension derives from an unresolved contradiction within us: we want her to get away with things, yet we want her to be cured; we are curious to know what the red flashes mean, yet we dread finding out; we want to know the truth, and want to suppress it. All of this corresponds to the tensions in Marnie herself. The urge towards cure is there from the start. We see it in the beautiful image of release that first shows us Marnie's face: she is washing her assumed personality (literally) out of her hair. The release is partial and mo- mentary, but clearly pleasurable: it epitomizes Marnie's need to find herself.

The constant general tension in which she lives—it is an existence from which all possibility of happiness or peace of mind is banished, a life of unrelieved precarious- ness—crystallises into detail at a few key moments. We have, at the race-track, the dialogue between Marnie and Mark about belief: dialogue casual and unconcerned, then plunging abruptly into intensity at a word that carries unexpected associations, builds up sudden emotional pressures: like the dialogue on the sand-dunes in *The Birds.* Marnie (it is just after she has been recognised as 'Peggy Nicholson', and has reacted with shock to the jockey's red-blotched shirt) says she doesn't believe in luck. Mark asks her what she *does* believe in. She replies, with a sudden intensity and bitterness, "Nothing", and the meaninglessness of her life as it is is brought home to us.

188

MARNIE: left, "Just wait till you've been victimised"; and right, Marnie re-enacts her crime.

It is significant, perhaps, in view of Hitchcock's supposed Catholic outlook, that what the ensuing remarks suggest she should believe in is relationships, not God.

It seems natural to link this with another moment where a similar particularizing of Marnie's tension occurs: the free association game. The scene is a superb example of Hitchcock's sureness of grasp, every point rendered with an exactness that by no means precludes complexity of attitude. We are not asked to take Mark as a profound psychologist; neither is he stupid. There is nothing intrinsically ridiculous in his reading psychological textbooks in order to explore his wife's condition more fully. Nor are we asked to believe that *Sexual Aberrations of the Criminal Female* gives him all—or any—of the answers. The whole point of the free association game is that it is Marnie's idea in the first place, and not only Marnie who initiates it, but Marnie who insists on prolonging it. All Mark has done is suggest she read some books and ask about her recurring dream. Certainly he wants to help her—wants to play amateur psychologist—but it is Marnie who insists on being helped. There is nothing abrupt or surprising about this. We have seen frequently in the film the possibility of a cure for Marnie. She is completely passive in Mark's arms, but at least she gives herself to them; in the beautiful sequence of three shots that closes Marnie's first visit to the Rutland home—the walk in long-shot across to the stable; the couple, still in long-shot, moving among the stalls; the close-up of the kiss—we are made to feel the possibility for Marnie of integration into a balanced, tranquil existence; the cut straight from her troubled look as she turns away from Mark to the scene of the theft, tells us that the crime, as committed, is an attempted flight from Mark—she feels her neurotic condition threatened by him. In the car, before he 'proposes', he, and we, accept her statement that she 'likes' him as perhaps more truthful than she knows. When she attempts suicide, it is in the ship's swimming-pool, not the sea: though the attempt is genuine enough, she is careful to preserve the *possibility* of being rescued. These intima-

190

tions of a desire to be helped crystallise in the 'Free association' scene.

The sequence opens with Marnie's dream, presenting the memory with greater immediacy and fidelity than hitherto. We see Marnie lying in a bed we haven't seen before, a cheap bed in a roughly furnished room, against a harshly blue pillow with 'Aloha' painted across it. The image fills us at once with unease because of its inexplicability: we don't know that what we see is a dream, nor do we know that this is the bed Marnie slept in as a child. What we see is the grown woman: a beautifully simple and direct depiction of the past's grip on the present. A hand taps on a window behind the bed-head; Marnie moans and tosses; the camera pans to the right and we pass from the child décor to the décor of Marnie's bedroom in the Rutland house (it was once Stella's, as the feminine décor and empty display cabinets have previously told us). Mark is now knocking on the door. He comes in, half arouses Marnie, who cringes away in terror: we get a subjective shot of his face, ominously dominating, very like the close-up of him as he overpowered her in the honeymoon sequence, his eyes boring into her. Then Lil comes in and succeeds in waking and calming her. After she goes, the idea of suicide is touched on (through the sleeping-pills: "The world is full of alternatives"), then Mark begins to ask about the dream. Marnie, almost caught off her guard, stops herself, looks at him, says, "You Freud—me Jane?" We see Mark in his chair: the low angle makes him look powerful, potentially dominating, but his attitude and expression suggest uncertainty. He asks her to read some of his books. She tells him she doesn't need to know how filthy men are, and adds, "In case you didn't recognise it, that was a rejection". But we know it wasn't: know especially from her questioning glance at him, but also from the very overemphasis of her speech—she is being deliberately provocative. 'Deliberately': but we have here a perfect example of that borderline between conscious

191

and subconscious intention, which makes 'deliberately' not quite the word. Using the same satirical tone she suggests and then insists on the free association: "Oh, doctor, I bet you're just dying to free associate": taunting as it is, it becomes an invitation to more than playing at psychology. He starts, awkwardly, she urges him on ("There. I'm not holding back at all, am I doctor?"). The word "sex" begins to break down her defences, although she still preserves the defensive-satirical tone ("Jack and Jill— you keep your filthy hands off me, Jack"). Death brings simply the association "me", and a feeble attempt to break off the game: we think of Marnie's declaration that she believes in "nothing", and remember her body floating in the pool. But Mark, encouraged, presses on with colours: "Black"—"White". Sudden low-angled shot of Mark, ominous and accusing with pointing finger: "Red" —and Marnie breaks down. The breakdown has been carefully prepared—and prepared partly by herself. She repeats "White—white": at once rejecting her own guilt and insisting on the whiteness—not redness—of the sailor's shirt: then collapses in Mark's arms with a cry of, "Oh, help me. Oh God, somebody help me". It is the moment, in fact, towards which the whole film has moved, from that first stiff walk along the deserted platform.

Much of the film's significance, and much of its emotional impact, is packed into the climactic cut of the flashback sequence from the child's screaming in the past to Marnie's scream in the present. Child and woman seem to face each other over the years, at the moment of experience and the moment of memory, and our awareness of the fragility and precariousness of life, of the miseries of human waste, of the tyranny of past over present, is most powerfully and movingly aroused. And after it Marnie's "There—there now", exact repetition of her words, expression and intonation when she shot Forio, is clearly addressed to more than the dead sailor: it is spoken to herself as child, to herself as woman; it is a laying of ghosts.

* * *

Marnie cannot pretend to the formal perfection of *Vertigo*. Its narrative, though logical enough in that it follows through the stages essential to Marnie's cure, is comparatively rambling and episodic; not everything arises naturally, as in *Vertigo,* from a single situation. It is quite possible, for example—even probable—that Marnie would ride with the hunt; that she would see the kill; that she would rush off suicidally; that Forio would fail to take the wall; but the sequence of events lacks inevitability, for all the sense of continuity given by the slow lap-dissolve that gives us Marnie's face lingering on from the previous ('cat-burglar') scene and suggests the continuance of her state of mind into the hunt episode, preparing us for her reactions. For all that, I am not sure that I prefer *Vertigo's* compact perfection to *Marnie's* relative looseness, which can be seen as reflecting a freedom new in Hitchcock. This is of all his films the one that most clearly formulates his moral position and most decisively, in a positive form, embodies his preoccupation with sexual relationships. With this freedom—to bring the argument of this chapter full circle—goes what has been condemned as carelessness or contempt for the audience, but is in fact merely a magnificent contempt for rules. The technical and formal freedom—the willingness to use any device, however conventionally dubious, to give each idea its most direct, most forceful, most economical expression, is but the outward manifestation of an ever freer creative flow, and *Marnie* is in many respects the satisfying culmination (to date: I do not wish to reject the possibility of further culminations beyond it) of the sequence begun by *Vertigo*.

1963 brought us films from three major directors that offered, in their very distinct ways, interesting parallels. Fellini's *8½,* Bergman's *Winter Light,* and *The Birds* all brought their central characters to the point of development where limiting, obstructive immaturities had to be cast off and fully responsible, fully adult life begun. This seemed to imply that the directors in question had set themselves a challenge—a problem as much human as artistic—especially in the cases of Fellini and Bergman, whose films suggested a closer relationship of director to protagonist than did Hitchcock's. With regard to Fellini's new film, we must not assume that way-out fantasy and a return to Giulietta Masina necessarily indicates flight or evasion. *The Silence* reveals progress, certainly, but it is progress still further downwards, a further ruthless demolition of humanist and religious assumptions that (for all the tentative gesture towards new life embodied in the child) leaves the positive work still to do. But with *Marnie* Hitchcock has responded to his own challenge magnificently, though in a devious, unexpected way. Perhaps the most disturbing and powerful factor in the effect of *Vertigo, Psycho* and *The Birds* lay in the sense they communicated of a precarious order in constantly imminent danger of being undermined by terrible destructive upsurgings from an underlying chaos. It is not absurd to compare this with the overturning of a similarly precarious order, with the resulting freeing of an uncontrollable, destructive 'under-nature' in the mature tragedies of Shakespeare. *Marnie* takes up again this assumption. Three varieties of order are set forth in the film: the neurotic order of Marnie's own life, rigidly held in place, constantly liable to irretrievable collapse; the order of the business world, materialistic, sterile, destructive of all human values; and the stagnant, over-tranquil order of Rutland Senior and his home—the tranquillity of a backwater. All three are exposed as inadequate, because all three are based on a rejection of the awareness of the underlying abysses, of human complexity and human needs, of the quicksands of identity. But in *Marnie* the underlying chaos finds an answer, and a logical one, in the film's endorsement of the implications of Mark Rutland's outlook and behaviour. Through him, a true order is defined, an order very difficult and dangerous to achieve but, in the Hitchcock universe, the only order tenable: an order arrived at through empiricism, flexibility, a trust in instinct that has its source in a basic sympathetic flow, a

194

rejection of all fixed rules, an acceptance of the necessary moral ambiguity of all positive action in an imperfect and bewildering world. Mark doesn't embody a positive force that can destroy the sense of precariousness and fragility —nothing can, and the film leaves us with the vulnerable children, potential Marnies, and their symbolic street-game. But he *does* embody an attitude towards it. *Marnie* may lack, to some extent, the formal perfection of other Hitchcock films, but it certainly does not mark a retrograde step in his development.

9. Torn Curtain

IT IS A pity that *Torn Curtain* is Hitchcock's fiftieth film: everyone expected a major landmark, a culmination. *The Birds,* despite weaknesses, was a culmination, and *Marnie* was another, beyond it. But *Torn Curtain* is no culmination, being unsatisfactory, episodic, lacking the really strong centre we have come to expect. Yet, though more loosely constructed than any other recent Hitchcock, it is more coherent than may be immediately apparent. No doubt those who found evidence of failing powers in *Marnie* will find more here, but three things should make them pause before delivering a verdict of senility: 1. *Torn Curtain,* uneven in tone and in intensity as it is, contains sequences as fine as any in Hitchcock. 2. In certain respects which I shall go into, it continues the remarkably swift and consistent development traceable through Hitchcock's last half dozen films. 3. The denigrators should have had time by now to realise, in retrospect, how wrong they were about *Marnie.*

The movement of *Torn Curtain* follows the archetypal Hitchcock pattern: first, a world of superficial order (an international scientific conference) from which the protagonists (and the spectator) are plunged into a world of chaos through which they must struggle towards a new stability. But Hitchcock, deciding to return, after *Marnie,* to one of his favourite genres, needed a hero essentially different from those of any of his comparable earlier adventure films: a hero active and dynamic who plunges into dangers from choice (and a new actor to play him—not Grant or Stewart, but the more aggressive and self-assertive Paul Newman).

The simplifications of popular fiction can, by a process of heightening and intensification, merge imperceptibly into myth. Like many heroes of mythology, Newman here sets out on a quest for something of vital importance; to get it and bring it back he must undergo various tests and ordeals. Again as with certain mythological heroes, the quest involves a descent into an underworld from which the object of the quest must be retrieved. What we have to deal with here, it had better be insisted at the outset, is not an allegory worked out in consistent detail, but a drama whose significance is frequently heightened by certain suggestive undertones. The credit title sequence presents us with inferno images: to the left of the screen, flame; to the right, dense smoke, from which faces anxious, distraught or tormented emerge and then disappear—faces we are to see later in the film. Only the faces of the lovers are calm and happy, and then only for the moment when they are shown together. In the penultimate sequence of the film the inferno idea recurs, the performance of *Francesca da Rimini* on stage being echoed in the auditorium, when Michael's cry of "Fire!" precipitates a mass panic that is the chaos-world in miniature. The action in the theatre parallels the action on stage: Paolo and Francesca menaced in hell by Guido; Michael and Sarah menaced in the seething hysterical mob by Gerhard. There are other hints in the film to support this view of it as a descent-and-quest myth. As the hero leaves on his quest, we are told (by the bookseller anxious about the condition of his religious section) to "pray for him"; Sarah accompanies Michael as a guardian angel ("I just knew I had to follow you, by instinct or to protect you . . ."); the members of Pye ("We are not a political organisation") are his guides in the underworld. We cannot say that East Germany is hell (or what is nice Professor

196

Lindt doing there?) but certainly it contains its lost souls, such as Gromek and the Countess Luchinska.

What is the object of the quest, what the nature of the underworld into which the hero descends, what (precisely) the dangers to which he exposes himself? Again, one must beware, with a film that strikingly lacks the extraordinary step-by-step logic of *Vertigo*, of suggesting that there is a symbolic or allegorical meaning that can be made to fit, point for point. No; but, again, there are overtones that make it clear we are dealing with something more than a simple thriller (if with something less than *Vertigo*). The answers to my questions can be approached through a further, related question: in what sense are Gromek and the Countess lost souls?—the Countess being entirely pathetic, Gromek more pathetic than sinister. They are lost because they belong nowhere; because they have no identity: both are displaced persons, Gromek with his constant nostalgia for America, the Countess with hers for Poland and her social class. Yet this is precisely the condition into which Michael *appears* to be descending during the first half hour of the film, and in which Sarah hovers on the point of joining him. It is true that he is only pretending, and she draws back in time from the brink; but the pretence involves endangering their relationship and it draws her towards the false position of sacrificing her own integrity in order to remain beside him. The pretence also involves him, and the spectator, in moral impurities that give most of the suspense sequences in the film their peculiar character— "suspense" being here, as always in Hitchcock, essentially a matter of moral tensions. I shall return to this later.

The object of the quest? Ostensibly a formula in the head of a Professor, a secret which will enable Michael to complete an "anti-missile missile" that will render (he claims) nuclear war impossible. However, what gets the emphasis is not the political but the *personal* importance of this formula. Michael's failure to perfect the missile has lost him the position at Washington that he feels would complete him: deprived of it, he is sinking into

TORN CURTAIN:
top, the press conference; and bottom, the killing of Gromek —aftermath.

a role he resents and feels unsuited to (teaching, instead of creating). The quest for the formula expresses, in a form almost diagrammatically neat, Michael's quest for that which will complete his sense of identity; and to gain it he must descend into a world where he exposes both himself and his *fiancée* to the most extreme dangers, moral as much as physical.

Closely connected with this, then, we find one of the clearest expressions of another recurrent Hitchcock theme: man's need to commit himself completely to a relationship with a woman, and not allow this relationship to be disrupted by doubts, secrets, concealments. At the opening of the film the hero's two basic needs are in direct conflict; the first half is concerned primarily with their reconciliation. Michael risks destroying his relationship with Sarah by refusing to be frank with her about what he is doing; it is only the strength of her fidelity that preserves it. The crucial development in the relationship—Michael's decision to tell her the truth—is precipitated by what is perhaps the one morally pure gesture in the film: her refusal during the preliminary interrogation to divulge, even for Michael's sake, what she knows about the missile. The fact that the characters are presented without much psychological detail is not a weakness: Hitchcock is giving us, in a pure and simplified form, all detail stripped away to give greater clarity to the essentials, a definition of fundamental human needs. For both, the relationship is crucial, yet for both it is necessarily subservient to something beyond it: for him the need to establish his identity finally through his work, for her, the need to preserve her personal integrity. Yet the relationship that appears at first sight to menace these higher needs is in fact vitally important to them. When the relationship is cemented by the removal of pretence and deceit, Sarah more than "protects": she saves Michael at exactly the moment when all seems lost, she proves herself indispensable to the success of his quest, for example by agreeing to talk with Lindt, by dancing with Karl while Michael manipulates Lindt into arranging a private meeting, by persuading Michael to help the Countess Luchinska, by drawing him, in the theatre, to the right door at the right moment. On the other hand, the spectator is made to feel that it is partly her ideal of Michael (which she thinks he has betrayed, yet to which he corresponds more closely than, at that time, she imagines) that gives her the strength to withstand her moment of trial at the interrogation. It is the love that made her waver that ultimately makes her stand firm.

The film, then, is built on strong foundations that have something of the essential simplicity of myth. But what gives it its particular pungent flavour—what acts as a veritable principle of composition, common to almost every episode—is Hitchock's sense of the necessary moral impurity of action in an imperfect world. The private relationship can be protected, to some extent, from this impurity: at the start of the film the lovers hide themselves from the world under blankets, at the end they again draw a blanket over their heads to screen themselves from a photographer, and at the film's turning-point, where Michael tells Sarah the truth, the kiss that seals their relationship is exchanged behind bushes. But as soon as there is involvement in the public world there is impurity. Sarah's act of moral integrity at the interrogation, by forcing Michael to reveal the truth to her, at once plunges her with him into the equivocal morality of his enterprise: she must begin lying, deceiving, tricking; and it is Sarah who persuades him to accept the Countess Luchinska's blackmail.

In some ways *Torn Curtain* refers us back to *Notorious* and *North by Northwest,* in both of which monstrous demands were made on the heroines in the name of political necessity. In *Torn Curtain* the morality of Michael's actions on the political level is called into question, though subtly and inexplicitly, throughout. He announces, at his first press conference, that he has defected in order to continue work on the anti-missile missile that will make nuclear war impossible. We reflect at once —and the presence of hostile reporters from the West

TORN CURTAIN: top, Professor Lindt, "A kindly, benign, delightful old gentleman"; and bottom, "The chaos-world in miniature."

encourages this—that in fact all the invention will do is make it possible for East to bomb West without fear of retaliation. When we learn the truth, this reflection obviously still stands, not perhaps conscious in the spectator's mind but there to trouble him just below the surface of consciousness: we have merely to reverse the sides.

Throughout the first part of the film the hero's course of action places him in a series of equivocal positions: especially, we watch his discomfiture at the press conference, under the questions from the reporters and, more particularly, the incredulous and accusing gaze of Sarah. But it is with the sequence of the killing of Gromek that the full bitter flavour of the film is tasted. It is of great importance that Hitchcock leads us into this sequence by revealing Michael's secret to us. We have spent the first half hour of the film in unattached bewilderment, knowing too little to identify with Paul Newman, yet too much to identify with Julie Andrews. At the moment when we learn the truth, our whole relationship to the film changes, we seize gratefully on Michael as hero: here is someone we can completely identify with. It is this involvement with a character, hence with a course of action, that makes the killing of Gromek the most disturbing murder in the whole of Hitchcock. The murder of Marion Crane shocked us, certainly; but at least we were taken by surprise, and had never *wanted* it. But here, as soon as Gromek reveals his presence, we say, "He will have to be killed," and, as the moments pass and nothing is done, this merges into "Go on—kill him." We are implicated—*we* are killing Gromek—and Hitchcock spares us no discomfort for our complicity. So many factors contribute to the effect of this rich and remarkable sequence. There is the sickening sense throughout of enforced commitment to actions that are unspeakably horrible—the presence of the farmer's wife is especially important in this respect, the culmination of the scene being the symbolic passing of blood from Michael's hand to hers as they try to wash it away. The horror is intensified by the fact that it is Gromek himself who forces them to kill him—he *wants* to die, placing himself in their power and then insistently provoking them. Hitchcock and his actor (Wolfgang Kieling, perhaps the finest performance in a film particularly rich in marvellously created minor roles) here convey, with that economy so characteristic of Hitchcock's films, the essence of a human being, in this case the sense of a man inwardly sickened by his own corruption. Hitchcock's method with Gromek (and it is repeated later with the Countess Luchinska) is to begin by arousing in the spectator a simple recoil of distaste (expressed on the screen for us in both cases by the reaction of Newman), and then, by making us feel the essential humanity of the character, to make us ashamed of our initial reaction. Finally, let me single out one other factor that contributes to the density of this sequence: the presence throughout it of the taxi driver, which intensifies the horror of what is happening by placing it in the context of the everyday. The disturbing effect of the sequence is clinched when Newman walks out of the farm kitchen that, homely and reassuring in appearance, has become a world of nightmare, to find the taxi driver still standing waiting for him, an innocent and unaware bystander.

The later episodes, it is true, yield nothing quite as dense in significance: no doubt the somewhat unsatisfactory total effect of *Torn Curtain* is partly due to the fact that it reaches its point of maximum intensity about a third of the way through and never quite regains it. There is, nonetheless, a great deal that is of interest in these later sequences. One notes, for example, a certain difference in tone between these and comparable episodes in earlier films. Hitchcock's films abound in vividly realized small parts; but here, each of the subsidiary characters seems conceived specifically to intensify in one way or another our sense of moral complexity—of moral *discomfort*. Consider for instance Michael's duel of wits with Professor Lindt. This formula for which the hero undertakes his descent into the underworld has to be wrested, not from a devil, not even from a lost soul, a Gromek, but from a kindly, benign, delightful old gentleman. Hence, at the moment of Michael's triumph, when the Professor exclaims "You told me nothing!" our sympathies are at least as much with him as with the film's hero. Or consider another particularly rich sequence, the 'bus journey (where back-projection, elsewhere in the film sometimes crude and ugly, achieves a notable expressive effect, intensifying the spectator's sense of the 'bus as a small enclosed world sealed off from the surrounding normality). Here, the presence of Fraulein Mann provokes the moral tension that is the essence of Hitchcockian suspense. On a superficial suspense level, her objections to helping Michael and Sarah threaten to jeopardize their escape; on a deeper level, she brings closer to the surface our doubts about the morality of the whole enterprise. Fraulein Mann's objection is that this time they are helping, not their fellow East Germans, but two foreigners, and Americans at that; and the partial validity of her objection brings to our consciousness the remembrance of what these Americans are escaping *with*. The lives of the 'bus "passengers"— and they include, by the end of the trip, one genuine passenger, an entirely innocent old woman—are being endangered to enable Michael to take back to America a formula that may destroy them all. We are also very much aware of the personal nature of his quest: in effect, these lives are being endangered for one man's selfish ambitions. When the departing Fraulein says that she hopes they get caught, our sympathies are not entirely against her.

The encounter with the Countess Luchinska is one of the film's most complex sequences in terms of moral implications. Her calling out his name to Michael in the street clearly constitutes a veiled threat: it is never certain that, if they reject her offer, she will not expose them. Our first response is to share Michael's distaste; but gradually we are led to dissociate ourselves from it as the pathos of her predicament is revealed. *Should* he accept? She is a silly and useless old woman who will scarcely be an asset to America, nor is America (to her

204

a dream world) likely to be of any use to *her:* she will be a displaced person anywhere, lost and wretched. But, as the scene progresses, we come to feel such compassion for her that we long for Michael to accept, and his hesitation seems priggish. He accepts, finally, for the wrong reason: not from compassion for a helpless and miserable old woman, but in order to be helped, and to remove the possibility that she will denounce them. Lila Kedrova is magnificent, with an extraordinary command of facial expression, gesture and intonation. But Hitchcock indulges her rather more than enough: one has too much the sense of an actress being allowed to "do her piece," and occasionally she is permitted to over-make points, as in her last utterance.

The episode in the theatre acts as an almost diagrammatically simple summing up of the whole film: Michael himself produces the chaos from which they must extricate themselves, with his cry of "Fire!"; torn apart, they are nearly lost in the seething anonymous crowds; finally, through their awareness of each other and thanks to Sarah's gaining the exit and drawing Michael to her, they escape, reunited. After which, the end is comparatively lightweight, a neatly executed Hitchcock suspense-joke, rather disappointing after all that has gone before. But one notes that even here the protagonists' escape is due not to a heroic or altruistic action, but to the desire of the stage-hand for payment—a motive scarcely more laudable than the petty vanity that causes the ballerina to denounce them. Our last glimpse of him is of a man alone, apart, greedily counting his money.

Torn Curtain is a remarkably rich film, yet one cannot escape, at the end, a certain sense of emptiness. This is partly due to what is in other ways so admirable—the undermining of the morality of what Michael is doing on a political level: we are left wondering what it has all been for, and not finding very much in the way of an answer. Worse, Hitchcock this time seems not greatly inspired by his principals—especially Julie Andrews, who is never more than adequate. The richness of the film lies, in fact, to a somewhat disproportionate degree in the vividness and complexity of the subsidiary characters and the use to which Hitchcock puts them: especially true of the latter half of the film, where the lovers occupy remarkably little of the spectators' attention, becoming, indeed, little more than pretexts for the various episodes, themselves uneven in complexity and interest. This leaves the film curiously without a firm centre. An interview published in Sweden when *Torn Curtain* opened there reveals that commercial pressures led Hitchcock to modify his original conception, by wrenching the Newman character at the last minute into a conventional hero-figure. The chief source of dissatisfaction with the film is, I think, our sense that we are being discouraged (unsuccessfully) from feeling the character to be as nasty as he in fact is. Although it contains much that one values, *Torn Curtain* as a whole is notably less successful than any other of Hitchcock's recent films.

Filmography

HITCHCOCK worked as assistant director and art director on: WOMAN TO WOMAN (Graham Cutts, 1923); THE WHITE SHADOW (Graham Cutts, 1923); THE PASSIONATE ADVENTURE (Graham Cutts, 1924); THE BLACKGUARD (Graham Cutts, 1925); THE PRUDE'S FALL (Graham Cutts, 1925).

NUMBER THIRTEEN. 1922. *Producer:* Alfred Hitchcock.

Players: Clare Greet, Ernest Thesiger.

Unfinished.

ALWAYS TELL YOUR WIFE. 1922.

Part co-directed with Seymour Hicks.

THE PLEASURE GARDEN. 1925. *Screenplay:* Eliot Stannard. *Based on the novel by:* Oliver Sandys. *Photography:* Baron Ventimiglia. *Production:* Gainsborough, Münchener Lichtspielkunst. 6,458 ft.

Players: Virginia Valli, Carmelita Geraghty, John Stuart.

THE MOUNTAIN EAGLE. 1926. *Screenplay:* Eliot Stannard. *Photography:* Baron Ventimiglia. *Production:* Gainsborough, Münchener Lichtspielkunst. 7,503 ft.

Players: Bernard Goetzke, Nita Naldi, Malcolm Keen.

THE LODGER. 1926. *Screenplay:* Alfred Hitchcock, Eliot Stannard. *Based on the novel by:* Mrs. Belloc Lowndes. *Photography:* Baron Ventimiglia. *Production:* Gainsborough. 7,685 ft.

Players: Ivor Novello, June, Marie Ault.

DOWNHILL. 1927. *Screenplay:* Eliot Stannard. *Based on a play by:* Ivor Novello and Constance Collier. *Photography:* Claude L. McDonnell. *Production:* Gainsborough. 8,635 ft.

Players: Ivor Novello, Ben Webster, Isabel Jeans.

EASY VIRTUE. 1927. *Screenplay:* Eliot Stannard. *Based on a play by:* Noël Coward. *Photography:* Claude L. McDonnell. *Production:* Gainsborough. 7,300 ft.

Players: Isabel Jeans, Franklin Dyall, Eric Bransby Williams.

THE RING. 1927. *Photography:* Jack Cox. *Production:* British International Pictures. 8,007 ft.

Players: Carl Brisson, Lillian Hall Davis, Ian Hunter.

THE FARMER'S WIFE. 1928. *Screenplay:* Eliot Stannard. *Based on the play by:* Eden Philpotts. *Photography:* Jack Cox. *Production:* British International Pictures. 67 minutes.

Players: Lillian Hall Davis, Jameson Thomas, Maud Gill.

CHAMPAGNE. 1928. *Screenplay:* Eliot Stannard. *Based on a story by:* Walter C. Mycroft. *Photography:* Jack Cox. *Production:* British International Pictures. 7,830 ft.

Players: Betty Balfour, Gordon Harker, Jack Trevor.

THE MANXMAN. 1928. *Screenplay:* Eliot Stannard. *Based on the novel by:* Sir Hall Caine. *Photography:* Jack Cox. *Production:* British International Pictures. 8,163 ft.

Players: Carl Brisson, Anny Ondra, Malcolm Keen.

Hitchcock's last silent film.

BLACKMAIL. 1929. *Screenplay:* Alfred Hitchcock, Benn W. Levy, Charles Bennett. *Based on a play by:* Charles Bennett. *Photography:* Jack Cox. *Production:* British International Pictures, 8,000 ft.

Players: Anny Ondra (with the voice of Joan Barry), Sara Allgood, John Longden.

ELSTREE CALLING. 1930. Part directed only. *Supervising Director:* Adrian Brunel. *Screenplay:* Val Valentine. *Photography:* Claude Friese-Greene. *Production:* British International Pictures. 7,770 ft.

Players: Anna May Wong, Donald Calthrop, Gordon Harker.

JUNO AND THE PAYCOCK. 1930. *Screenplay:* Alfred Hitchcock, Alma Reville. *Based on the play by:* Sean O'Casey. *Photography:* Jack Cox. *Production:* British International Pictures. 85 minutes.

Players: Sara Allgood, Edward Chapman, Maire O'Neill.

MURDER. 1930. *Screenplay:* Alma Reville. *Based on the play* Enter Sir John *by:* Clemence Dane and Helen

Simpson. *Photography:* Jack Cox. *Production:* British International Pictures. 92 minutes.

Players: Herbert Marshall, Norah Baring, Phyllis Konstam.

Hitchcock also directed a German language version of this film with Alfred Abel and Olga Tchekowa.

THE SKIN GAME. 1931. *Screenplay:* Alfred Hitchcock. *Based on the play by:* John Galsworthy. *Photography:* Jack Cox. *Production:* British International Pictures. 85 minutes.

Players: Edmund Gwenn, Jill Esmond, John Longden.

RICH AND STRANGE. 1932. *Screenplay:* Alma Reville, Val Valentine. *Based on a theme by:* Dale Collins. *Photography:* Jack Cox, Charles Martin. *Production:* British International Pictures. *Release:* Wardour. 83 minutes.

Players: Henry Kendall, Joan Barry, Percy Marmont.

NUMBER SEVENTEEN. 1932. *Screenplay:* Alfred Hitchcock. *Based on the play and novel by:* Jefferson Farjeon. *Photography:* Jack Cox. *Production:* British International Pictures. *Release:* Wardour. 5,766 ft.

Players: Léon M. Lion, Anne Grey, John Stuart.

LORD CAMBER'S LADIES. 1932. *Producer:* Alfred Hitchcock. *Director:* Benn W. Levy.

WALTZES FROM VIENNA. 1933. *Screenplay:* Alma Reville, Guy Bolton. *Based on a play by:* Guy Bolton. *Production:* Tom Arnold. *Release:* G.F.D. 80 minutes.

Players: Jessie Matthews, Esmond Knight, Frank Vosper.

THE MAN WHO KNEW TOO MUCH. 1934. *Screenplay:* A. R. Rawlinson, Edwin Greenwood. *Based on an original theme by:* Charles Bennett, D. B. Wyndham-Lewis. *Photography:* Curt Courant. *Production:* Gaumont British. *Release:* G.F.D. 74 minutes.

Players: Leslie Banks, Edna Best, Peter Lorre.

THE THIRTY-NINE STEPS. 1935. *Screenplay:* Alma Reville, Charles Bennett. *Based on the novel by:* John Buchan. *Photography:* Bernard Knowles. *Production:* Gaumont British. *Release:* G.F.D. 87 minutes.

THE SECRET AGENT. 1936. *Screenplay:* Charles Bennett. *Based on a play by:* Campbell Dixon. *Adapted from* Ashenden *by:* W. Somerset Maugham. *Photography:* Bernard Knowles. *Production:* Gaumont British. *Release:* G.F.D. 83 minutes.

Players: Madeleine Carroll, John Gielgud, Peter Lorre.

SABOTAGE. 1936. *Screenplay:* Charles Bennett. *Based on the novel* The Secret Agent *by:* Joseph Conrad. *Photography:* Bernard Knowles. *Production:* Gaumont British. *Release:* G.F.D. 77 minutes.

Players: Sylvia Sidney, Oscar Homolka, John Loder.

YOUNG AND INNOCENT. 1937. *Screenplay:* Charles Bennett, Alma Reville. *Based on a novel by:* Josephine Tey. *Photography:* Bernard Knowles. *Production:* Gainsborough. *Release:* G.F.D. 84 minutes.

Players: Nova Pilbeam, Derrick de Marney, Percy Marmont.

THE LADY VANISHES. 1938. *Screenplay:* Sidney Gilliat, Frank Launder. *Based on the novel* The Wheel Spins *by:* Ethel Lina White. *Photography:* Jack Cox. *Production:* Gainsborough. *Release:* Gaumont British. 97 minutes.

Players: Margaret Lockwood, Michael Redgrave, Paul Lukas.

JAMAICA INN. 1939. *Screenplay:* Sidney Gilliat, Joan Harrison. *Based on the novel by:* Daphne du Maurier. *Photography:* Harry Stradling, Bernard Knowles. *Production:* Mayflower Pictures. *Release:* A.B.P.C. 108 minutes.

Players: Charles Laughton, Maureen O'Hara, Leslie Banks.

REBECCA. 1940. *Screenplay:* Robert E. Sherwood, Joan Harrison. *Based on the novel by:* Daphne du Maurier. *Photography:* George Barnes. *Art Director:* Lyle Wheeler. *Editor:* Hal C. Kern. *Music:* Franz Waxman. *Producer:* David O. Selznick. *Production:* Selznick International. *Release:* United Artists. 130 minutes.

Players: Laurence Olivier *(Max de Winter),* Joan Fontaine *(Mrs. de Winter),* George Sanders *(Jack Favell),* Judith Anderson *(Mrs. Danvers),* Nigel Bruce *(Major Giles*

Lacey), C. Aubrey Smith *(Colonel Julyan)*, Reginald Denny, Gladys Cooper, Florence Bates.

FOREIGN CORRESPONDENT. 1940. *Screenplay:* Charles Bennett, Joan Harrison. *Photography:* Rudolph Maté. *Special Effects:* Lee Zavitz. *Art Directors:* William Cameron Menzies, Alexander Golitzen. *Editors:* Otto Lovering, Dorothy Spencer. *Music:* Alfred Newman. *Producer:* Walter Wanger. *Production/release:* United Artists. 120 minutes.

Players: Joel McCrea *(Johnnie Jones)*, Laraine Day *(Carol Fisher)*, Herbert Marshall *(Stephen Fisher)*, George Sanders *(Herbert Folliott)*, Albert Basserman *(Van Meer)*, Robert Benchley *(Stebbins)*, Eduardo Cianelli *(Krug)*, Edmund Gwenn *(Rowley)*, Harry Davenport *(Mr. Powers)*.

MR. AND MRS. SMITH. 1941. *Screenplay:* Norman Krasna. *Based on an original story by:* Norman Krasna. *Photography:* Harry Stradling. *Special Effects:* Vernon L. Walker. *Art Directors:* Van Nest Polglase, L. P. Williams. *Editor:* William Hamilton. *Music:* Roy Webb. *Producer:* Harry E. Edington. *Production/release:* RKO. 95 minutes.

Players: Carole Lombard *(Ann Smith)*, Robert Montgomery *(David Smith)*, Gene Raymond *(Jeff Custer)*, Jack Carson *(Chuck Benson)*, Philip Merivale *(Mr. Custer)*, Lucile Watson *(Mrs. Custer)*, William Tracy *(Sammy)*, Charles Halton, Esther Dale, Emma Dunn.

SUSPICION. 1941. *Screenplay:* Samson Raphaelson, Joan Harrison, Alma Reville. *Based on the novel* Before the Fact *by:* Frances Iles. *Photography:* Harry Stradling. *Special Effects:* Vernon L. Walker. *Art Director:* Van Nest Polglase. *Editor:* William Hamilton. *Music:* Franz Waxman. *Production/release:* RKO. 99 minutes.

Players: Cary Grant *(John Aysgarth)*, Joan Fontaine *(Lina MacKinlaw)*, Nigel Bruce *(Beaky)*, Sir Cedrick Hardwicke *(General MacKinlaw)*, Dame May Whitty *(Mrs. MacKinlaw)* Isabel Jeans *(Mrs. Newsham)*, Heather Angel, Auriol Lee, Reginald Sheffield, Leo. G. Carroll.

SABOTEUR. 1942. *Screenplay:* Peter Viertel, Joan Harrison, Dorothy Parker. *Based on an original idea by:* Alfred Hitchcock. *Photography:* Joseph Valentine. *Art*

Director: Jack Otterson. *Editor:* Otto Ludwig. *Music:* Charles Prévin, Frank Skinner. *Producer:* Frank Lloyd. *Production/release:* Universal. 109 minutes.

Players: Robert Cummings *(Barry Kane),* Priscilla Lane *(Patricia Martin),* Otto Kruger *(Charles Tobin),* Alan Baxter *(Mr. Freeman),* Alma Kruger *(Mrs. Van Sutton),* Vaughn Glazer, Dorothy Peterson, Ian Wolfe, Anita Bolster.

SHADOW OF A DOUBT. 1943. *Screenplay:* Thornton Wilder, Alma Reville, Sally Benson. *Based on a story by:* Gordon McDonnell. *Photography:* Joseph Valentine. *Art Directors:* John B. Goodman, Robert Boyle, R. A. Gausman, L. R. Robinson. *Editor:* Milton Carruth. *Music:* Dimitri Tiomkin. *Producer:* Jack H. Skirball. *Production/release:* Universal. 108 minutes.

Players: Joseph Cotten *(Charlie Oakley),* Teresa Wright *(Charlie Newton),* Macdonald Carey *(Jack Graham),* Patricia Collinge *(Emma Newton),* Henry Travers *(Joseph Newton),* Hume Cronyn *(Herbie Hawkins),* Wallace Ford *(Fred Saunders),* Janet Shaw, Estelle Jewell, Eily Malyon, Ethel Griffies.

LIFEBOAT. 1943. *Screenplay:* Jo Swerling. *Based on a story by:* John Steinbeck. *Photography:* Glen MacWilliams. *Art Directors:* James Basevi, Maurice Ransford. *Editor:* Dorothy Spencer. *Music:* Hugo Friedhofer. *Producer:* Kenneth MacGowan. *Production/release:* 20th. Century-Fox. 96 minutes.

Players: Tallulah Bankhead *(Constance Porter),* William Bendix *(Gus Smith),* Walter Slezak *(Willy),* Mary Anderson *(Alice Mackenzie),* John Hodiak *(John Kovac),* Henry Hill *(Charles D. Rittenhouse),* Heather Angel *(Mrs. Higgins),* Hume Cronyn *(Stanley Garett),* Canada Lee *(George Spencer).*

BON VOYAGE. 1944. *Screenplay:* J. O. C. Orton, Angus McPhail. *Based on an original idea by:* Arthur Calder-Marshall. *Photography:* Gunther Krampf. *Art Director:* Charles Gilbert. *Production:* M.O.I.

Players: John Blythe, the Molière Players.

ADVENTURE MALGACHE. 1944. *Photography:* Gunther Krampf. *Art Director:* Charles Gilbert. *Production:* M.O.I.

Players: The Molière Players.

SPELLBOUND. 1945. *Screenplay:* Ben Hecht. *Based on the novel* The House of Dr. Edwardes *by:* Francis Beeding, *adapted by:* Angus McPhail. *Photography:* George Barnes. *Special Effects:* Jack Cosgrove. *Art Directors:* James Basevi, John Ewing. *Dream sequences designed by:* Salvador Dali. *Editors:* William Ziegler, Hal C. Kern. *Music:* Miklos Rozsa. *Producer:* David O. Selznick. *Production:* Selznick International. *Release:* United Artists. 111 minutes.

Players: Ingrid Bergman *(Dr. Constance Peterson),* Gregory Peck *(John Ballantine),* Jean Acker *(The Directress),* Rhonda Fleming *(Mary Carmichael),* Donald Curtis *(Harry),* John Emery *(Doctor Fleurot),* Leo G. Carroll *(Doctor Murchison),* Norman Lloyd *(Garmes),* Steven Geray, Paul Harvey, Erskine Sandford, Janet Scott.

NOTORIOUS. 1946. *Screenplay:* Ben Hecht. *Based on a theme by:* Alfred Hitchcock. *Photography:* Ted Tetzlaff. *Special Effects:* Vernon L. Walker, Paul Eagler. *Art Directors:* Albert S. D'Agostino, Carol Clark, Darrell Silvera, Claude Carpenter. *Editor:* Theron Warth. *Music:* Roy Webb. *Producer:* Alfred Hitchcock. *Production/release:* RKO. 102 minutes.

Players: Ingrid Bergman *(Alicia Huberman),* Cary Grant *(Devlin),* Claude Rains *(Alexander Sebastian),* Louis Calhern *(Paul Prescott),* Leopoldine Konstantine *(Mrs. Sebastian),* Reinhold Schünzel *(Dr. Anderson),* Moroni Olsen, Ivan Triesault, Alexis Minotis.

THE PARADINE CASE. 1947. *Screenplay:* David O. Selznick. *Based on the novel by:* Robert Hichens, *adapted by:* Alma Reville. *Photography:* Lee Garmes. *Art Directors:* Joseph McMillan, Thomas N. Morahan. *Editors:* Hal C. Kern, John Faure. *Music:* Franz Waxman. *Producer:* David O. Selznick. *Production:* Selznick International. 110 minutes.

Players: Gregory Peck *(Anthony Keane),* Ann Todd *(Gay Keane),* Charles Laughton *(Judge Horfield),* Ethel

Barrymore *(Lady Sophie Horfield)*, Charles Coburn *(Sir Simon Flaquer)*, Louis Jourdan *(André Latour)*, Alida Valli *(Maddalena Anna Paradine)*, Leo G. Carroll, Isabel Elsom, Pat Aherne.

ROPE. 1948. *Screenplay:* Arthur Laurents. *Based on the play by:* Patrick Hamilton, *adapted by:* Hume Cronyn. *Photography:* (Technicolor): Joseph Valentine, William V. Skall. *Art Director:* Perry Ferguson. *Editor:* William H. Ziegler. *Music:* Leo F. Forbstein, *based on a theme by:* Poulenc. *Producer:* Sidney Bernstein. *Production:* Transatlantic Pictures. *Release:* Warner Brothers. 81 minutes.

Players: James Stewart *(Rupert Cadell)*, Farley Granger *(Philip)*, John Dall *(Shaw Brandon)*, Joan Chandler *(Janet Walker)*, Sir Cedric Hardwicke *(Mr. Kentley)*, Constance Collier *(Mrs. Atwater)*, Edith Evanson *(Mrs. Wilson)*, Douglas Dick *(Kenneth Lawrence)*, Dick Hogan *(David Kentley)*.

UNDER CAPRICORN. 1949. *Screenplay:* James Bridie. *Based on the novel by:* Helen Simpson, *adapted by:* Hume Cronyn. *Photography:* (Technicolor): Jack Cardiff, Paul Beeson, Ian Craig, David McNeilly, Jack Haste. *Art Director:* Thomas N. Morahan. *Editor:* A. S. Bates. *Music:* Richard Adinsell. *Producer:* Sidney Bernstein. *Production:* Transatlantic Pictures. *Release:* Warner Brothers. 116 minutes.

Players: Ingrid Bergman *(Lady Henrietta Flusky)*, Joseph Cotten *(Sam Flusky)*, Michael Wilding *(Charles Adare)*, Margaret Leighton *(Milly)*, Jack Watling *(Winter)*, Cecil Parker *(the Governor)*, Dennis O'Dea *(Corrigan)*, Olive Sloane, John Ruddock, Bill Shine, Victor Lucas.

STAGE FRIGHT. 1951. *Screenplay:* Whitfield Cook. *Based on two stories by:* Selwyn Jepson, *adapted by:* Alma Reville. *Photography:* Wilkie Cooper. *Art Director:* Terence Verity. *Editor:* Edward Jarvis. *Music:* Leighton Lucas. *Producer:* Alfred Hitchcock. *Production:* A.B.P.C. *Release:* Warner Brothers. 110 minutes.

Players: Marlene Dietrich *(Charlotte Inwood)*, Jane Wyman *(Eve Gill)*, Michael Wilding *(Inspector Wilfred Smith)*, Richard Todd *(Jonathan Cooper)*, Alastair Sim

(Commodore Gill), Sybil Thorndike *(Mrs. Gill),* Kay Walsh, Miles Malleson, André Morell, Joyce Grenfell.

STRANGERS ON A TRAIN. 1951. *Screenplay:* Raymond Chandler, Czenzi Ormonde. *Based on the novel by:* Patricia Highsmith, *adapted by:* Whitfield Cook. *Photography:* Robert Burks. *Special Effects:* H. F. Koene Kamp. *Art Directors:* Edward S. Haworth, George James Hopkins. *Editor:* William H. Ziegler. *Music:* Dimitri Tiomkin. *Producer:* Alfred Hitchcock. *Production/release:* Warner Brothers. 101 minutes.

Players: Farley Granger *(Guy Haines),* Ruth Roman *(Anne Morton),* Robert Walker *(Bruno Anthony),* Leo G. Carroll *(Senator Morton),* Patricia Hitchcock *(Barbara Morton),* Laura Elliott *(Miriam Haines),* Marion Lorne *(Mrs. Anthony),* Jonathan Hale *(Mr. Anthony),* Howard St. John, John Brown, Norma Varden, Robert Gist, John Doucette.

I CONFESS. 1952. *Screenplay:* George Tabori, William Archibald. *Based on a play by:* Paul Anthelme. *Photography:* Robert Burks. *Art Directors:* Edward S. Haworth, George James Hopkins. *Editor:* Rudi Fehr. *Music:* Dimitri Tiomkin. *Producer:* Alfred Hitchcock. *Production/release:* Warner Brothers, 95 minutes.

Players: Montgomery Clift *(Father Michael Logan),* Anne Baxter *(Ruth Grandfort),* Karl Malden *(Inspector Larrue),* Bryan Aherne *(Willy Robertson),* O. E. Hasse *(Otto Keller),* Dolly Hass *(Alma Keller),* Roger Dann *(Pierre Grandfort),* Charles André *(Father Millais),* Judson Pratt *(Murphy),* Ovila Legare *(Villette),* Gilles Pelletier *(Father Benoit).*

DIAL M FOR MURDER. 1954. *Screenplay:* Frederick Knott. *Based on the play by:* Frederick Knott. *Photography* (Warnercolor, 3-D): Robert Burks. *Art Directors:* Edward Carrere, George James Hopkins. *Editor:* Rudi Fehr. *Music:* Dimitri Tiomkin. *Producer:* Alfred Hitchcock. *Production/release:* Warner Brothers. 105 minutes.

Players: Ray Milland *(Tony Wendice),* Grace Kelly *(Margot Wendice),* Robert Cummings *(Mark Halliday),* John Williams *(Inspector Hubbard),* Anthony Dawson

(Captain Swan Lesgate), Leo Britt *(the narrator)*, Patrick Allen *(Pearson)*, George Leigh *(Williams)*, George Alderson *(the detective)*, Robin Hughes *(Police Sergeant)*.

REAR WINDOW. 1954. *Screenplay:* John Michael Hayes. *Based on a novelette by:* Cornell Woolrich. *Photography* (Technicolor): Robert Burks. *Special Effects:* John P. Fulton. *Art Directors:* Hal Pereira, Joseph McMillan Johnson, Sam Comer, Ray Mayer. *Editor:* George Tomasini. *Music:* Franz Waxman. *Producer:* Alfred Hitchcock. *Production/release:* Paramount. 112 minutes.

Players: James Stewart *(L. B. Jefferies)*, Grace Kelly *(Lisa Fremont)*, Wendell Corey *(Thomas J. Doyle)*, Thelma Ritter *(Stella)*, Raymond Burr *(Lars Thorwald)*, Judith Evelyn *(Miss Lonely Hearts)*, Ross Bagdasarian *(the composer)*, Georgine Darcy *(Miss Torso)*, Jesslyn Fax *(Miss Hearing Aid)*, Rand Harper *(Honeymooner)*, Irene Winston *(Mrs. Thorwald)*, Denny Bartlett, Len Hendry, Mike Mahoney, Alan Lee, Anthony Warde, Harry Landers.

TO CATCH A THIEF. 1955. *Screenplay:* John Michael Hayes. *Based on the novel by:* David Dodge. *Photography* (Technicolor): Robert Burks. *Special Effects:* John P. Fulton. *Art Directors:* Hal Pereira, Joseph McMillan Johnson, Sam Comer, Arthur Krams. *Editor:* George Tomasini. *Music:* Lyn Murray. *Producer:* Alfred Hitchcock. *Production/release:* Paramount. 107 minutes.

Players: Cary Grant *(John Robie)*, Grace Kelly *(Frances Stevens)*, Charles Vanel *(Bertani)*, Jessie Royce Landis *(Mrs. Stevens)*, Brigitte Auber *(Danielle Foussard)*, René Blancard *(Commissioner Lepic)*, John Williams, Georgette Anys, Roland Lesaffre, Jean Hebey, Dominique Davray, Russell Gaige, Marie Stoddard, Frank Chellano.

THE MAN WHO KNEW TOO MUCH. 1955. *Screenplay:* John Michael Hayes, Angus McPhail. *Based on a story by:* Charles Bennett, D. B. Wyndham-Lewis. *Photography* (Technicolor): Robert Burks. *Special Effects:* John P. Fulton. *Art Directors:* Hal Pereira, Henry Bumstead, Sam Comer, Arthur Krams. *Editor:* George Tomasini. *Music:* Bernard Herrmann. *Lyrics:* Jay Livingston,

Ray Evans. *Cantata "Storm Cloud" by:* Arthur Benjamin, D. B. Wyndham-Lewis. *Producer:* Alfred Hitchcock. *Production:* Filwite Productions. *Release:* Paramount. 119 minutes.

Players: James Stewart *(Dr. Ben McKenna),* Doris Day *(Jo, his wife),* Daniel Gelin *(Louis Bernard),* Brenda de Banzie *(Mrs. Drayton),* Ralph Truman *(Inspector Buchanan),* Mogens Wieth *(The Ambassador),* Alan Mowbray *(Val Parnell),* Hillary Brooke *(Jan Peterson),* Christopher Olsen *(Little Hank McKenna),* Reggie Nalder *(Rien, the assassin),* Yves Brainville, Richard Wattis, Alix Talton, Noel Willman, Carolyn Jones, Leo Gordon, Abdelhaq Chraibi, Betty Bascomb, Patrick Aherne, Louis Mercier, Anthony Warde, Lewis Martin, Richard Wordsworth.

THE TROUBLE WITH HARRY. 1956. *Screenplay:* John Michael Hayes. *Based on the novel by:* Jack Trevor Story. *Photography* (Technicolor): Robert Burks. *Special Effects:* John P. Fulton. *Art Directors:* Hal Pereira, John Goodman, Sam Comer, Emile Kuri. *Editor:* Alma Macrorie. *Music:* Bernard Herrmann. *Song* "Flagging the Train to Tuscaloosa" *music by:* Raymond Scott. *Lyrics by:* Mack David. *Producer:* Alfred Hitchcock. *Production/ release:* Paramount. 99 minutes.

Players: Edmund Gwenn *(Captain Albert Wiles),* John Forsythe *(Sam Marlowe),* Shirley MacLaine *(Jennifer),* Mildred Natwick *(Miss Gravely),* Jerry Mathers *(Arnie),* Mildred Dunnock *(Mrs. Wiggs),* Royal Dano *(Calvin Wiggs),* Parker Fennelly, Barry Macollum, Dwight Marfield, Leslie Wolff, Philip Truex, Ernest Curt Bach.

THE WRONG MAN. 1957. *Screenplay:* Maxwell Anderson, Angus McPhail, *Based on* The True Story of Christopher Emmanuel Balestrero *by:* Maxwell Anderson. *Photography:* Robert Burks. *Art Directors:* Paul Sylbert, William L. Kuehl. *Editor:* George Tomasini. *Music:* Bernard Herrmann. *Producer:* Alfred Hitchcock. *Production/ release:* Warner Brothers. 105 minutes.

Players: Henry Fonda *(Christopher Emmanuel Balestrero),* Vera Miles *(Rose, his wife),* Anthony Quayle *(O'Conner),* Harold J. Stone *(Lieutenant Bowers),* Charles

Cooper *(Matthews, a detective)*, John Heldabrand *(Tomasini)*, Richard Robbins *(Daniel)*, Esther Minciotti, Doreen Lang, Laurinda Barrett, Norma Connolly, Nehemiah Persoff, Lola D'Annunzio, Kippy Campbell, Robert Essen, Dayton Lummis, Frances Reid, Peggy Webber.

VERTIGO. 1958. *Screenplay:* Alec Coppel, Samuel Taylor. *Based on the novel* D'Entre les Morts *by:* Boileau and Narcejac. *Photography* (Technicolor): Robert Burks. *Special Effects:* John P. Fulton. *Art Directors:* Hal Pereira, Henry Bumstead, Sam Comer, Frank McKelvey. *Editor:* George Tomasini. *Music:* Bernard Herrmann. *Producer:* Alfred Hitchcock. *Production/release:* Paramount. 128 minutes.

   Players: James Stewart *(John "Scottie" Ferguson)*, Kim Novak *(Madeleine Elster, Judy Barton)*, Barbara Bel Geddes *(Midge)*, Henry Jones *(The Coroner)*, Tom Helmore *(Gavin Elster)*, Raymond Bailey *(The Doctor)*, Ellen Corby, Konstantin Shayne, Lee Patrick.

NORTH BY NORTHWEST. 1959. *Screenplay:* Ernest Lehman. *Photography* (Technicolor): Robert Burks. *Special Effects:* A. Arnold Gillespie, Lee Leblanc. *Art Directors:* Robert Boyle, William A. Horning, Merrill Pye, Henry Grace, Frank McKelvey. *Editor:* George Tomasini. *Music:* Bernard Herrmann. *Producer:* Alfred Hitchcock. *Production/release:* MGM. 136 minutes.

   Players: Cary Grant *(Roger Thornhill)*, Eva Marie Saint *(Eve Kendall)*, James Mason *(Phillip Vandamm)*, Jessie Royce Landis *(Clara Thornhill)*, Leo G. Carroll *(The Professor)*, Philip Ober *(Lester Townsend)*, Josephine Hutchinson *(The Housekeeper)*, Martin Landau *(Leonard)*, Adam Williams *(Valerian)*, Carleton Young, Edward C. Platt, Philip Coolidge, Doreen Lang, Edward Binns, Robert Ellenstein, Lee Tremayne, Patrick McVey, Ken Lynch, Robert B. Williams, Larry Dobkin, Ned Glass, John Beradino, Malcolm Atterbury.

PSYCHO. 1960. *Screenplay:* Joseph Stefano. *Based on the novel by:* Robert Bloch. *Photography:* John L. Russell. *Special Effects:* Clarence Champagne. *Art Directors:* Joseph Hurley, Robert Clatworthy, George Milo. *Editor:*

George Tomasini. *Music:* Bernard Herrmann. *Producer:* Alfred Hitchcock. *Production/release:* Paramount. 108 minutes.

Players: Janet Leigh *(Marion Crane)*, Anthony Perkins *(Norman Bates)*, Vera Miles *(Lila Crane)*, John Gavin *(Sam Loomis)*, Martin Balsam *(Milton Arbogast)*, John McIntire *(Sheriff)*, Simon Oakland *(Dr. Richmond)*, Frank Albertson *(the millionaire)*, Patricia Hitchcock, Vaughn Taylor, Lurene Tuttle, John Anderson, Mort Mills.

THE BIRDS. 1963. *Screenplay:* Evan Hunter. *Based on the story by:* Daphne du Maurier. *Photography* (Technicolor): Robert Burks. *Special Effects:* Lawrence A. Hampton. *Art Directors:* Robert Boyle, George Milo. *Editor:* George Tomasini. *Sound Consultant:* Bernard Herrmann. *Producer:* Alfred Hitchcock. *Production/release:* Universal. 120 minutes.

Players: Rod Taylor *(Mitch Brenner)*, Tippi Hedren *(Melanie Daniels)*, Jessica Tandy *(Mrs. Brenner)*, Suzanne Pleshette *(Annie Hayworth)*, Veronica Cartwright *(Cathy Brenner)*, Ethel Griffies *(Mrs. Bundy)*, Charles McGraw *(Sebastian Sholes)*, Ruth McDevitt *(Mrs. MacGruder)*, Joe Mantell, Malcolm Atterbury, Karl Swenson, Elizabeth Wilson, Lonny Chapman, Doodles Weaver, John McGovern, Richard Deacon, Doreen Lang, Bill Quinn.

MARNIE. 1964. *Screenplay:* Jay Presson Allen. *Based on the novel by:* Winston Graham. *Photography* (Technicolor): Robert Burks. *Art Directors:* Robert Boyle, George Milo. *Editor:* George Tomasini. *Music:* Bernard Herrmann. *Producer:* Alfred Hitchcock. *Production/release:* Universal. 130 minutes.

Players: Tippi Hedren *(Marnie Edgar)*, Sean Connery *(Mark Rutland)*, Diane Baker *(Lil Mainwaring)*, Martin Gabel *(Sidney Strutt)*, Louise Latham *(Bernice Edgar)*, Bob Sweeney *(Cousin Bob)*, Alan Napier *(Mr. Rutland)*, S. John Launer *(Sam Ward)*, Mariette Hartley *(Susan Clabon)*, Bruce Dern, Henry Beckman, Edith Evanson, Meg Wyllie.

TORN CURTAIN. 1966. *Screenplay:* Brian Moore. *Photography* (Technicolor): John F. Warren. *Art Directors:*

Frank Arrigo, Hein Heckroth, George Milo. *Editor:* Bud Hoffman. *Music:* John Addison. *Producer:* Alfred Hitchcock. *Production/release:* Universal. 128 minutes.

Players: Paul Newman *(Michael Armstrong),* Julie Andrews *(Sarah Sherman),* Lila Kedrova *(Countess Kuchinska),* Hansjöerg Felmy *(Heinrich Gerhard),* Tamara Toumanova *(Ballerina),* Wolfgang Kieling *(Hermann Gromek),* Günter Strack *(Professor Karl Manfred),* Ludwig Donath *(Professor Gustav Lindt),* David Opatoshu *(Mr. Jacobi),* Gisela Fischer *(Dr. Koska),* Mort Mills *(Farmer),* Carolyn Conwell *(Farmer's Wife),* Arthur Gould-Porter *(Freddy),* Gloria Gorvin.

TOPAZ. 1969. *Screenplay:* Brian Moore. *Based on the novel by:* Leon Uris. *Photography* (Technicolor): Jack Hildyard. *Art Director:* Alexander Golitzen, Henry Bumstead. *Producer:* Alfred Hitchcock. *Production/release:* Universal.

Players: Frederick Stafford, John Forsythe, Tina Hedstrom, Dany Robin, Claude Jade. Philippe Noiret, Michel Piccoli.

Bibliography

Books and Pamphlets

Bogdanovich, Peter. *The Cinema of Alfred Hitchcock* (Museum of Modern Art Film Library/Doubleday & Co. Inc., New York, 1962).

Douchet, Jean. *Hitchcock* (Cahiers de l'Herne, Paris, 1965).

Amengual, Barthélémy, and Borde, Raymond. *Alfred Hitchcock* (Premier Plan, SERDOC, Lyon, 1960).

Manz, Hans-Peter. *Alfred Hitchcock* (Sanssouci Verlag, Zürich, 1962).

Perry, George. *The Films of Alfred Hitchcock* (Studio Vista Ltd., London, 1965).

Rohmer, Eric, and Chabrol, Claude. *Hitchcock* (Editions Universitaires, Paris, 1957).

Truffaut, François. *Le Cinema selon Hitchcock* (Robert Laffont, Paris, 1966. English translation entitled *Hitchcock*: Simon and Schuster, New York, 1968; Martin Secker and Warburg, London, 1968).

Articles and Interviews

Anderson, Lindsay. *The Films of Alfred Hitchcock.* (Sequence 9, London. Autumn 1949).

Bitsch, Charles, and Truffaut, François. *Rencontre* (Cahiers du Cinéma, Number 62, Paris, August-September 1956).

Cameron, Ian. *Hitchcock and the Mechanics of Suspense* (Movie, Numbers 3 and 6, London, October 1962 and January 1963).

—, and Jeffery, Richard. *The Universal Hitchcock* (Movie, Number 12, London, Spring 1965).

—, and Perkins, V. F. *Interview with Alfred Hitchcock* (Movie, Number 6, London, January 1963).

Domarchi, Jean. *Le Fer dans la Plaie* (Cahiers du Cinéma, Number 63, Paris, October 1956).

Douchet, Jean. *La Troisième Clef* (Cahiers du Cinéma, Number 99, Paris, September 1959).

Houston, Penelope. *The Figure in the Carpet* (Sight and Sound, London, Autumn 1963).

Pechter, William S. *The Director Vanishes* (Moviegoer, Number 2, New York, Summer-Autumn 1964).

Perkins, V. F. *Rope* (Movie, Number 7, London, February-March 1963).

Complete issue of Cahiers du Cinéma, Number 39, October 1953, devoted to Hitchcock, with articles by Bazin, Chabrol, Astruc, and Truffaut. Also see Number 62, August-September 1956.